EVEN THE SIDEWALK COULD TELL

EVEN

THE SIDEWALK

COULD TELL

How I Came Out to My Wife,
My Three Children, and the World

ALON OZERY

REGENT PARK PUBLISHING

Hardcover ISBN: 978-1-5445-2471-9
Paperback ISBN: 978-1-5445-2469-6
eBook ISBN: 978-1-5445-2470-2

CONTENTS

INTRODUCTION

It All Starts with Three Steps

A few years ago, I travelled to New York City. It was my first visit, and I was in awe of all the buildings and the energy of the city.

One afternoon, I decided to go see Grand Central Station, at the heart of the city on 42nd Street. It was just after five as I left the station and headed towards the city centre. I was still thinking about Grand Central as I approached the pedestrian light to cross Madison Avenue. I looked up and saw that the light was red. As my eyes moved down from there, I suddenly realized that there was a wall of people across the street, all waiting to cross. It made sense; the workday was done, and they were all rushing to get to the station and go home.

It struck me that there must be a couple hundred people standing there, and I was about to be directly in their path. It seemed there would be no way for me to get through this wall of people, with everyone standing so close to one another. There appeared to be not even an inch between one person and the next. I looked up the street and thought that perhaps I should walk a block further up to avoid this human wall that I was about to collide with.

But then I thought, *No, I'm not walking around this one. I'm going to cross the street right here and now.* I thought this even though I didn't really see how it would be possible to make my way through the crowd, like a tiny fish floating upstream amid a sea of much larger creatures. Resolved, I still felt a little nervous as I waited for the light to turn green.

And then, there it was. Hesitantly, taking my first step, I lifted my right foot and started to walk forward. I had no confidence that I wasn't about to be run over by this gang of people, dressed in their professional best. As I took my second step, I made a decision. I dropped my shoulders, straightened my back, and lifted myself up to my full height. As soon as I did that, my posture had a bit more energy to it. I looked forward intently, focussing on getting to the pavement on the other side of the street. Even though I had doubt in my heart, I didn't allow it to show. The wall advanced closer to me. For each step I took forward, they moved forward as well. And then, when I took the third step, I spotted a small gap in the wall.

I moved towards that gap with confidence and intent. As if the wall could read my mind, the gap grew bigger and bigger. I continued walking towards it and quickly arrived at the opening. Oddly, a path was forming with every step I took. It wasn't a perfect path, but it was definitely forming before my very eyes. My shoulder bumped into a couple of other shoulders, and I had to take a couple of turns before I arrived at my destination—but I made it.

When I got to the other side of Madison Avenue, I stopped, turned around, and looked at the crowd, now moving farther and farther away. My path had already been swallowed up. I realized that the path had revealed itself simply because of my presence—almost as if I had willed it to exist.

As I looked back, I wondered what would have happened if I hadn't taken those first three steps forward. What if I had just stood there on the other side of the road, waiting for a path to form? Well, obviously, it wouldn't have.

People would have walked around this odd-looking guy, standing immobile on the pavement.

And then the light would have turned red again.

What if I had walked a block farther up the street? Again, obviously, the path would not have formed. Possibly, I would have just stood in front of another wall of people, only at a slightly different junction.

The only way the gap and then the path would form was by my taking those first few steps and trusting that the path would open. The more confident I appeared, the faster that path would appear and the wider it would become.

This is a book about getting off the sidewalk, taking those first few steps forward, and waiting for the path to open up before you—even when you can't see how that's possible.

CHAPTER ONE

Roots

My parents come from very different backgrounds, yet they both rebelled against their upbringing by marrying each other.

My dad was born into an Orthodox Jewish family that lived in the centre of Jerusalem. As an affluent business owner and a rabbi, my grandfather was considered a leader in the community. The family lived in a large two-story house with not only my dad's family but also some extended family.

My dad grew up following the Jewish Orthodox lifestyle to the letter. This didn't leave a lot of room for free thought. For instance, if you were to ask anyone in my dad's family why it wasn't okay to use electricity during the Sabbath, they would respond that the reason was because the Bible doesn't allow for work on the Sabbath and creating light is work. If you were to respond that turning on the light switch didn't feel like work to you, the conversation would quickly end with something like this: "Well, it's because tradition doesn't allow it. Period. Just follow the rules." You get the point, I'm sure.

The thing about my dad is that as he grew up, he didn't follow the rules. He left home at an early age and ended up in Canada in his late twenties, where he fell in love with and married a young, freckled English nurse. Horror of all horrors, she wasn't Jewish!

My mom was born into a very wealthy Protestant (but not religious) family in a beautiful, affluent village in Kent, England. My mom's father was a successful builder, and he ensured that the family had plenty of "help," a tennis court, a car, and abundant opportunities to travel the world. Even with all this privilege, my mom and her siblings were raised in a Victorian culture that demanded children be seen and not heard.

While my grandpa spent all of his time and energy growing the business, my colourful and energetic grandma kept herself well occupied. She definitely stood out and was certain that she had what it took to perform. At one point, she even recorded an opera album. Let's just say that while grandma had no shortage of the charisma and flair necessary for opera, she did lack the voice for it. That didn't stop her, though. I remember her busting out in operatic song during our visits to see her when I was a child. Even as a kid, I knew she wasn't very good, but I was drawn to her energy and desire to be the centre of attention, no matter the means. It's interesting to me that my mom and her siblings turned out to be the opposite of their mother. Unlike their mother, the kids were all fairly introverted and preferred not to be in the spotlight.

In her early twenties, my mom left England on the *Queen Mary*. She landed in Canada, where she began working as a nurse. It was there that she met a brown-skinned man with a funny accent. On top of that, he was Jewish! I can only imagine my grandma's face when she heard the news. My mom ultimately converted to Judaism, but not at the Orthodox level.

My two younger brothers and I were born in Canada. I was the first, and then my brothers—Guy and Aharon—followed in quick succession, each of us a year apart. When I was born, my parents thought I was perfect. Although my parents broke away from the presumed natural course of their lives, not everything about their past was erased. My mother served as the main caregiver to my brothers and I, and we inherited some of the Victorian principles she had been raised on. My mom had escaped the stiff-lipped culture she was brought up in and rebelled against her upbringing by moving away and marrying into a completely different culture, yet she had tremendous internal strife. She was a very talented artist yet was afraid to show her art.

Just a few years after my brothers and I were born, our family moved to Israel. The fact that our mother wasn't born Jewish was one of those topics that was never spoken about directly. Even though my dad broke the rules by going against his family's religion, he still loved and respected his family and his religion. Throughout my childhood in Israel, my family spent one weekend per month in Jerusalem from sundown on Friday through sundown on Saturday recognizing the Sabbath.

That freckled English nurse I like to call Mom was named Pamela Elisabeth, but our religious family called her Ruth. Only later in life did I make the connection that Ruth was King David's mother; she was also a convert. At the time, I also didn't know that all female converts were renamed Ruth. Looking back through the eyes of an adult, I can see that for this and so many other reasons, our life in Israel must have been a massive cultural shock for my mom. For example, there were two dining tables at my grandfather's house, one in the living room and another in the dining room. In the centre of the dining room was a large, long table that seated at least twelve people. This was the men's table. The women's table was tucked out of the way, next to the balcony door in the living room. Even though there were more than four women in my family, the table only sat four. It was assumed that the women were so busy making and serving the food that they would take turns sitting and sneaking in a quick bite before the next woman took her turn to eat.

Mom really tried to fit in, even though I'm sure it took a toll on her. I still remember overhearing a heated exchange in Yemeni Arabic between my dad's uncle and another family member. I asked my dad what they were talking about. He dismissed the conversation as nothing more than family gossip, but I knew they were speaking about my mom. The adults all thought they were being secretive about the conflicting feelings they had about my mom's Christian roots and her not-up-to-Orthodox-standards conversion—but it was a badly kept secret. It was just part of our life.

Despite some rocky moments like that, most of my childhood was peaceful. We moved around a lot within the same area, a middle-class village surrounded by fields and orange and pecan groves. My brothers and I spent most of our days playing outside. Together, we were noisy and fairly wild. Of the three of us, I was most like my mom. I'm sure that being the first child of three also had an effect on me. I was naturally the most responsible sibling and always did what I thought was expected of me—until I didn't. But more about that later on.

Without my brothers, I was different, though. Sometimes I still have flashbacks to how shy I was as a child when I was left to my own devices without my brothers nearby. Grade two specifically stands out in that regard. I had just one friend and was terrified of people I didn't know to the extent that when guests visited and the doorbell rang at home, I ran into my parents' room and hid under their bed.

The fact that I was bullied by a kid at school that same year didn't help. Looking back, I would give him a four out of ten for his bullying skills. He put some effort into harassing me, but he certainly didn't give it his all. He never went out of his way to find me, but on the occasions when he saw me walking in the school corridor, he would push me into a wall. One time, he closed the classroom door on my finger. My intense scream and authentically broken finger gave me a holiday from my bully. It lasted for about a month, after which point, he resumed his bullying by shoving me. However, by the time we hit grade three, he had lost interest in bullying me.

I was a legitimately asthmatic kid, but I used those respiratory issues to my advantage, pretending to have asthma attacks to convince my mom I needed to stay home. I think I missed a quarter of the school year in grade two. After that, I developed a pattern of using sickness as an excuse to get out of uncomfortable or scary situations. One time, I was chosen to be a bush in the school play and was scared to death about being onstage for everyone to see. As the day of the performance drew closer, I actually developed a fever. I'm sure I made myself sick, and I could not have been more relieved about that fact. I hid out from other things, too, such as performing, speaking, or any other school-related activity that would draw attention to me. Despite the relief I felt at the time, looking back, I can see how I put chains on myself as a child through this kind of self-imposed isolation. Over time, this behaviour developed into a pattern of running and hiding from life rather than dealing with it.

As I grew older, I got better at socializing, but I constantly fixated on how the people around me thought I should behave and whether I was meeting their expectations. Those expectations I perceived others as having served as my guiding light. Because of this, I had friends, but they were the kind of friendships in which no real conversations took place. We just did things together. This was on me. I always kept an air of distance between myself and others, which prevented me from developing close friendships. Also, each of my friends was from a different circle, so I never really hung out with groups of people. When I did find myself in large groups, I generally stayed quiet, with the exception of spouting off occasional one-liners. There was also the fact that my family moved around throughout Israel, from one town to the next. I never stayed at one school for more than two years.

My dad was a partner in two different companies, and my family always belonged to the upper middle class. One of those companies was a fairly successful T-shirt company that distributed its products across the country. The second company, which my dad ran with a partner, specialized in importing unique branded gifts that companies would give to their employees. That business always seemed glitzy to me, with its headquarters located in a lavish beachfront Sheraton Hotel in Tel Aviv.

Israel fell into financial turmoil in the 1980s, when the Israeli currency was devalued not once but twice. Although I didn't make the connection at the time, it was because of this that my mom and dad told my brothers and me that we were moving to Canada in thirty days' time. I was sixteen and had just finished grade ten. My parents explained that the financial prospects in Israel weren't good and we needed a new start. My brothers and I didn't know it at the time, but I later learned that my dad was forced to close the T-shirt business because of the economy. In their attempt to save the company, my parents sold our house so they could invest the money in the business. It didn't work. We had nothing, and the banks would be all over us if we didn't leave quickly.

With little warning or ceremony, my brothers and I were ripped away from the warm Middle Eastern culture we had always known. We were accustomed to living near the Mediterranean, where we enjoyed warm summers and nice, moderate winters. Now here we were, suddenly being uprooted to a foreign and frigid Anglo-Saxon country.

A few days before my family left for Canada, I rode my bicycle around our neighbourhood. I stopped on a small hill that allowed me to look down at our house and most of the neighbourhood. A sense of nostalgia crept over me. Throughout my life, I have experienced similar moments during times of transition—that feeling that the end of a chapter is upon me even as I am still in the midst of it.

It's funny because as hard as it was to leave Israel, I also knew at that moment on that hill that the ensuing move was aligned with what had to be. I knew it was the right decision, even though it required me to leave behind everything I had ever known. Looking back, I wonder if maybe this feeling of rightness had something to do with the fact that my subconscious knew I wasn't really connected to my surroundings or the people in my life because I wasn't connected to who I was.

CHAPTER TWO

Oh, Canada

My family landed in Toronto with nothing but our suitcases. We spent the first few months living with family and then moved to a small bungalow of our own in a middle-class neighbourhood. We also got a secondhand Lada, a boxy car from Russia that I was deeply embarrassed by. On the days my dad drove my brothers and me to school, we insisted that he drop us off a couple of blocks away so that our classmates wouldn't see us. The school was located in a fairly affluent area, and most of the other kids our age were driving their own Golf GTI convertibles.

Shortly after we moved into our new home, I decided I needed to find a part-time job. My parents never asked my brothers and me to work, but we didn't have much money, and I wanted the ability to buy nice things for myself. One afternoon, I walked to a small strip mall plaza located on the main street. The first door I came upon was a small but bustling Jewish deli called Coleman's. Up until then, I had only known Canadian food as burgers, pizza, and hot dogs. Suddenly before me was a whole world of Jewish traditions right here in North America: corned beef, pastrami, knishes, latkes. It was all there. The smell of steaming brisket filled the entire restaurant.

I walked up to the cash register, where a young guy greeted me. My hesitation and nervousness must have clued him in to the fact that I wasn't a customer. He introduced himself as Steven. Little did I know how lucky I was that he was filling in for the student who was supposed to work that day. I also didn't know that this marked the official beginning of my long career in food.

It was a red-banner day for me because that day in Coleman's, I also learned something about myself that continues to be true: when I want something, I have the ability to get it without overcomplicating things like I normally do. I can just go out, knock on doors, and get what I want. As an adult, I can recognize that as one of my strong suits. Sometimes I get a no, but rejection doesn't bother me because I've learned that every negative response gets me that much closer to a yes.

I was hired as a dishwasher, and a few months later, both of my brothers began working at Coleman's too. The job provided us with spending money and also meant that we could contribute to the family money pot when necessary. With that first taste of financial freedom, I was determined to be successful. To be honest, this desire to succeed would prove to be a great burden as the years went on. The drive to succeed took first place on my priority list. I discovered that I loved buying myself brandname clothes. I wanted people to see that I could afford to buy them. There were other things about myself that I *didn't* want people to see, so perhaps in some ways I used the veil of success and everything that came with it to divert people's attention (and my own) away from other issues.

But of course, I didn't yet know all of this when I started at Coleman's, back in the days when bread and red meat weren't yet the root of all evil.

In some ways, Coleman's introduced me to a bigger world. It was there that I had my first encounter with a gay person. Terri, the front-of-house manager, was a happy guy who liked his booze and his Latin guys. Every few months, Terri's latest boyfriend would join Coleman's waitstaff just as Terri's previous boyfriend disappeared. I noticed that Terri's and his boyfriend's lives seemed to involve a lot of drinking. Other than that, they all seemed nice enough, but I had nothing in common with them.

Work, school, and my emerging drive to succeed didn't leave a lot of time or energy for dating. Before my family moved to Canada, I noticed that a couple of girls suddenly hung out around me more than they had before. While I noticed, I didn't think too much about it. Then one of them began writing to me when I moved to Canada. I liked her and responded, but the exchange didn't last long. Maybe because I sprayed my mom's perfume on my letters to her?

During my two years in high school in Toronto, I had a few other encounters with girls. I was so lonely in this new, large high school that I welcomed friendship of any variety, platonic or romantic. A cute girl of Czech descent started visiting me at Coleman's. We ended up going out a few times, and then one night she invited me to her house. Bon Jovi played on her tape deck as we talked over a glass of wine. So sophisticated. In the middle of the conversation, as "Bad Medicine" thrummed in the background, I suddenly found myself being wrestled down onto the carpet, pinned under this girl. I think we kissed.

What I remember most about that night is feeling incredibly uncomfortable. To this day, I still sort of think that I owe this girl a bouquet of flowers and an apology for that evening because I feel as if I led her on. I wanted to spend time with her, but not in a romantic way. I never expressed that, though—probably because I generally liked the idea of having a girlfriend, despite the fact that I felt nothing for this specific girl. To me, our relationship felt like having a girlfriend in a play. She was right there next to me, but what was happening wasn't for real. I wanted a girlfriend, but not enough to make it happen. More specifically, I was never attracted enough to a girl to make it happen.

There were other close encounters, though. Another time, I was on a break at school, roaming through the corridors and looking for a quiet place where I could spend the long forty minutes until my next class began. I often looked for escapes at school to avoid empty conversations with students who knew me only from the classes we shared. One of these sanctuaries existed at the end of the school building, next to the gym and janitor's room. Few students used the stairs over there, and I loved the dimly lit, cool, and quiet space. I spent my time in the stairwell either reading a book or getting lost in my own thoughts as I daydreamt about being somewhere else. Usually that involved faraway places I hadn't been to that I could only assume were idyllic, if not perfect.

As I opened the door to walk into the stairwell that day, I noticed someone behind me. It was an outgoing Muslim girl who wore a hijab. I knew her from one of my classes. She had always been chatty and nice to me, but I had never really thought much about it.

My heart fell as she waved. *Shit, now I will have to talk to her,* I thought. Still, not wanting to be impolite, I waved. Then I let the door close behind me.

Undeterred by the closed door, she followed me into the stairwell and approached with a smile on her face. "How are you doing, Alon?" she asked.

"I'm good," I replied, perfectly cool. "What are you doing here?"

"Oh, just looking for a quiet place to chill. Can I chill with you?" she asked.

I was so uncomfortable, but I said, "Sure."

She appeared to take my response as a cue to come even closer. I had nowhere to escape, thanks to the table that was randomly placed in the stairwell, blocking my exit. *Who put this fucking table here anyway?* I wondered.

She continued moving closer and closer until she closed in on me, wrapping her arms around me. I began to sweat lightly, which I always do when I'm uncomfortable. She tried to kiss me. When her face was just a few centimetres away from mine, I frantically wiggled out of her reach.

My heart was pumping as I walked quickly towards the door, apologizing and saying that I really needed to go. As I walked away, all I could think about was how pissed I was that my sanctuary was no longer safe and now I had to find a new one.

Needless to say, that girl never talked to me again.

CHAPTER THREE

Army Life

I grew up and came of age with a mishmash of Israeli, Canadian, and British influences, but because I spent my formative years in Israel and immigrated to Canada with my family just after my sixteenth birthday, my army service was mandatory. In Israel, all boys join the army for three years, and girls for two years, upon turning eighteen or graduating from grade twelve. My family and I all accepted that I would go back to Israel to join the army when I was of age, so that's exactly what I did two years after moving to Toronto.

I graduated from high school in June and then spent the summer working at the deli so that I would have some money both for the flight back to Israel and to keep me financially afloat for my first few months there. The summer flew by as most summers do, and I booked a ticket for early October. I didn't have many friends left in the town that I grew up in, and it felt as if I was starting a completely new chapter in my life, even though I had lived in Israel before. My aunt and uncle who lived in Jerusalem opened their home to me. They did not have any children, and I felt very comfortable with them.

Within one month, I was enlisted and became the property of the Israeli Army for the next three years.

Shortly after arriving on base, I was called in to meet with a panel of placement officers who would determine where I would be placed for the next three years. I knew I wouldn't be in a combat role based on my asthma, but the placement still felt like a big deal to me, just like it did for all of us, because a young soldier's role affects their aspirations and social status.

When the time came, I stood in line waiting to be interviewed by three placement officers. My future—or, at the very least, the next three years of it—was in their hands. At that moment, their decision meant everything to me. I felt good about my prospects. I spoke fluent English and had graduated high school. I felt that I could make a positive contribution to the system.

As the time ticked by and my turn in front of the placement officers neared, a knot of nervous excitement formed in the pit of my stomach. I wondered if they would place me in a top-secret intelligence unit. Or perhaps they would assign me to be a liaison with English-speaking units.

Finally, my name was called, and I walked up the wooden stairs into a large room. A ceiling fan turned ever so slowly, barely having an effect on the unbearable heat.

The room was bare except for a long desk, where three middle-aged officers sat very still, as if they were trying to avoid any unnecessary movement, lest it might cause them to sweat. They barely seemed to notice my entrance. After what seemed like a long time, the officer on the far right side of the table lifted his gaze towards me. "Your name, soldier?" he asked.

"Alon Ozery, sir," I replied.

I waited for what felt like forever (but was probably just a few seconds), staring at a spot just above their heads. The army would prepare me well for staring and waiting.

"Okay, soldier, you have three options," the officer said at last. I looked him directly in the eye at that point, and I'm sure my anticipation must have been clear as day. "The first option is general office work. The second is to work in a warehouse. And the third is to serve as a truck driver."

I remained silent, feeling as if I had been punched in the stomach.

"Which one will it be?" the officer impatiently prompted me.

A heavy weight seemed to settle deep inside of me. It felt as if I was being pulled down and it was suddenly a struggle to stand up straight. "Is that it?" I finally asked.

"Yes, soldier. What will it be? We don't have all day."

Once again, I looked him directly in the eye as I spoke. "But I can do so much more," I explained, believing there must have been some sort of mistake. "I've completed all of my science courses, and I speak fluent English."

"You are a soldier, not a civilian. You do what you are told." I was pretty sure that I detected a snarky note in his tone. "Which one will it be?" he prompted again.

A fire of rebellion ignited within me at that moment. *Fuck you!* I thought. "I choose none of those options, sir." With that, I turned around and left. Before turning, I noticed that one of the officers wrote something down next to my name. I felt victorious, like I had really given it to them. *That'll show them!* I thought. *They can't treat me like that.*

Well, as it turned out, they *could* treat me like that.

I spent the next three months in a special section of basic training that was designed for asthmatics. I must say that none of us looked like elite soldiers, but we did the best we could. We spent our days being instructed to run around different trees on the base. Most of the time, about 30 percent of the soldiers waited it out on the sidelines because they had a doctor's note that excused them from running. We felt like pretend soldiers.

Our closing ceremony took place on a Thursday night. We all put on our good uniforms and gathered at eight, with all our belongings in tow, just as we had been asked to.

When the ceremony ended, our commander called each of us by name and directed us towards one of the several buses parked nearby. None of us knew what was going on or where we were headed. I had quickly learned that this was typical army protocol: just follow the rules and don't ask questions. My mind ran wild as I was directed to one of the buses. *Where am I going?* I wondered. After all, I hadn't agreed to be assigned to any position.

Upon entering the bus, I was greeted by a rough crowd. These guys would certainly never be mistaken for being university-bound. On my way to my seat, I asked a few of them if they knew where we were going. Each of them told me that they had asked to be a truck driver. As I sat down, the reality of my situation began to set in. I was going to be among this group of people for the rest of my time in the service. It turned out that the army had decided I would be a truck driver, one of the lowest-status jobs available. It was usually reserved for problematic young men.

I would fight this verdict. This was not what I had come to the army for. I had come to maximize my potential.

A couple of hours later, the bus entered a large army base that, no surprise, was full of trucks. When we got off of the bus, we were greeted by a poorly dressed army officer who was missing two front teeth. As he began to speak, it was clear that his grammar was poor too.

After he finished talking to the group, I walked over to him and let him know that since I would not be staying in this position for long, I wouldn't be partaking in the driving lessons.

He laughed in response. "No problem with me, brother," he said. "You can stay on this base for three years and just wait."

I followed the rest of the group as we were assigned to our rooms and claimed our beds. I locked my bag and sleeping bag to my bed with a padlock and ventured to the restroom. When I returned to my bed, I found that my sleeping bag was gone. It had been stolen, which meant I had to pay a fine to get a new one. *Can anything else go wrong?* I wondered as I sat on the bed with my head buried in my hands.

In that moment, I felt desperately alone and acutely aware of the fact that my parents were an ocean away. As I sat there, the book *Catch-22* popped into my head. It is simultaneously one of the funniest and most depressing books I've ever read, and it's all about how the army makes no sense. The plot revolves around a soldier who wants to claim that he is crazy in order to avoid combat. The problem is that army rules state that a soldier doesn't qualify as crazy for not wanting to go into battle.

In that moment, I had an epiphany: from then on, I would do whatever I could to fight this big army machine. It clearly didn't care about me, and therefore, I wouldn't care about it. I got out of my bed and headed out to wait for a bus to arrive with other new recruits. I waited while they disembarked and then walked into their rooms and grabbed the first unsecured sleeping bag I saw.

I succeeded in never driving a truck for the entire time I was on base. I used all my connections and, within a couple of months, was moved to another unit, where I became a youth instructor. That was a much more suitable job for me.

I very quickly understood that the army was senselessly bureaucratic, and I spent most of my time there fighting the system. The logic of large systems never worked for me. A decision made for masses of people rarely addresses the needs of all. I understand that this is how organizations work and that most people comply. Up until I joined the army, I was one of these compliant people, but serving in the military awoke the rebel in me.

Towards the end of my service, the command centre summoned all of the youth instructors for a three-day educational seminar. I arrived at the base early in the morning on the first day of the seminar and, after talking to a few people, realized how futile these next few days would be. Each day would start with the commanders talking about regulations, rules, and more rules, followed by lectures from uninspiring educators. Whenever I sit in a classroom setting, my mind begins to drift, and I find myself snapping out of it at the end of class without any memory of what we discussed. I think this was one of the reasons I never did well in school. Any setting where I have to listen to a monotonous presenter sends me to other worlds.

I decided to get out of the seminar.

A year before that seminar, I had been sitting on a bus eavesdropping on two soldiers. One of them was enthusiastically talking about how he had gotten out of his chores by faking asthma attacks. His friend smiled and asked him if he had asthma. "No. I just fake them," the first soldier replied.

I leaned in closer, pretending to stretch. I didn't want to miss the next part.

"I light a match and inhale the smoke the sulfur creates," he explained. "It works every time!" Genius.

That conversation popped back into my head as I thought about how much I didn't want to attend the seminar that day. As I devised a game plan, I headed over to visit a friend of mine who worked in one of the offices at the base. I found her sitting amid all the grey and olive-green furniture that the army loves to use, her face glazed over with boredom. She had just finished the important work of making coffee for her commander.

"Hey, can I have your matches, please?" I asked her.

"But you don't smoke," she replied, looking confused. "And you have asthma." Still, she handed me the matches.

"Come see something," I told her, smiling. I was excited to put the information the universe had so generously provided me to use for the first time. After I induced an asthma attack, my plan was to walk over to the base doctor, who would surely send me home for the day. It was a hot summer day, and I figured I might even be able to make it to the beach before noon. Suddenly, my day looked much more appealing than when I'd presumed I would spend it sitting in an unairconditioned room, listening to boring lectures alongside a hundred other sweaty soldiers, all wearing hot, olive-green uniforms.

My friend looked at me intently. "Do you think this is a good idea?" she asked, clearly concerned.

"I'm not sure," I replied honestly. "I've never tried this before." With that, I counted to three in my head, exhaled, lit the match, and inhaled the smoke. Within seconds, my lungs reacted to the smoke. A strong wheeze escaped from my lungs. Success! I instinctively placed my hand on my front pocket to make sure my inhaler was there. I never went anywhere without it, and it had saved me many, many times in the past. After a few more breaths, I felt that I could handle the wheezing. It sounded worse than it was—perfect!

My friend looked worried. "Are you okay?" she asked. "Maybe this wasn't a good idea."

"Thanks for your help!" I said with a smirk and a wheeze. "I'm going to see the doctor now. Tell the commander I'm not feeling well."

Soldiers looked at me as I walked down the corridor and out of the building to the infirmary, which was located just a couple of minutes away in a small building not far from the base's entrance. As I approached the building, I saw a lineup of about fifteen soldiers, all waiting outside the doctor's door to see him. I was wheezing heavily at this point, and the looks of sympathy directed my way gave me the courage to walk past the line and up to the closed door. Once I reached it, I placed my left arm dramatically on the side of the door as if I need support to keep myself from falling. Nobody from the line said a word to me as I knocked on the door. This was good. Israelis usually get very aggressive when it comes to line-cutters.

The door opened and I was greeted by a clearly annoyed young medic. "Wait your turn, soldier!" she barked. But then she noticed the wheezing and pulled me into the office. The doctor lifted his eyes from the person sitting in front of him. Within seconds, that patient was kicked out, and I was placed on a khaki-coloured hospital bed. The medic listened to my chest, and I lied and told her that I had breathed into my inhaler and it wasn't working. She conferred with the doctor in the corner of the room.

Perfect! I thought. It was only nine. I would rest a little, and everything would settle down. I estimated that I would be out of there by eleven with a note that would give me a couple of days off. I would be at the beach just after noon.

As I laid on the bed, I saw the medic approaching me with an IV. A wave of fear washed over me. I don't like needles at all. The fear must have made it look as if I was doing worse because a worried look crossed the medic's face, and she moved towards me faster. "Shirt off. Arm out," she directed tersely.

I was still wheezing, and I'm sure I was also pale by that point, thanks to the thought of the needle entering my arm. I turned my head in the other direction so that I wouldn't have to see the needle. I felt several pricks in my arm. I could see from out of the corner of my eye that blood was dripping from my arm onto the floor. I felt like I was going to faint from the sight. I suddenly noticed how very young the medic appeared to be. *Is this her first day as a medic? Did she just graduate from her medic course? Can't she find my vein?* Eventually, she got it right.

The doctor came over and looked at me. I'm sure I must have looked (and sounded) like a mess by that point. He assured me that the IV would calm me down. "You'll feel better within the hour, soldier," he said.

My breath began to settle back into a normal rhythm, and the fear I'd felt about the needle and dripping blood dissipated. Things were going my way! Thoughts of the beach drifted back into my head.

The doctor began seeing other soldiers in the next room. Within about thirty minutes, another medic entered the room. The doctor returned, and the three of them whispered among themselves, glancing my way every once in a while. I didn't give it a second thought; I was too busy congratulating myself for beating the system. It occurred to me that maybe I would get three days off instead of two!

The new medic walked over to my bed and asked me how I was doing. I was still wheezing a bit, but it was subsiding. "I'm feeling better. Thanks," I assured him.

"Okay, young man. You'll be coming with me," he said, and he began rolling my stretcher towards the door.

"What? Where? But I'm feeling better!"

He swung the door open, and that's when I saw that an ambulance was backed up to the doctor's office, with its rear doors wide open, waiting to swallow me in. I had nothing else to say.

The ambulance drove frantically through the busy city streets, with its siren blaring the entire time. *This is actually kind of cool,* I thought. *Everyone is moving out of the way just for me!* When we arrived at the hospital, the ER doctor took a quick look at me and didn't give me much attention beyond that. It was as if he knew I was faking. Maybe he did. I was released within a couple of hours and—sure enough—I got the next three days off. I made it to the beach after all. A little later than I had planned, but I still made it.

By the time I entered the army, I had enough self-awareness to understand not only that I have the tendency to be a cynical smart-ass but also that this tendency worked against me. Still, sometimes I couldn't help myself.

One day, we youth instructors had a group meeting with our direct commander. This guy was a bureaucrat who felt very comfortable working in the army. He followed orders and expected soldiers to follow his orders. But he was a good guy. He had called us together to let us know that our unit was going to be audited by central command. This was problematic because we were an administrative mess and behind on many formalities, such as making sure all the daily reports were complete and filed properly or making sure that all our class presentations were properly written out and colour coded. Our commander knew this, and he wanted us to be as prepared as possible for the audit.

Today, I understand that this is a normal scenario. A team is behind and an audit is on the horizon, so it's time for the team to get their shit together. But back then, as I sat in the meeting, all I could see was that our commander was making mistakes. It was the perfect scenario for me to shoot off some of my snarky, cynical comments, and I couldn't help myself. I could see that my negative comments were annoying the commander, but even that didn't stop me.

The following weekend, I was on guard duty at our central command. I was bored and somehow found myself in my commander's office, going through his drawers. A few months prior, I had applied to become an instructor of a lucrative course that required good English skills—*check*! It also required experience working with youth—*check*! I was the perfect fit for this program, and I knew it. I was sure that I would be accepted. As I was rifling through my commander's drawer, I came upon a list of names, a few of which I knew. Somewhere in the middle of the list, I saw a name crossed out. My name. Suddenly it dawned on me how hurtful my comments had actually been. Hurtful enough that he had gone through the effort of going back to his office and crossing my name off the list, even though I was perfect for the course and wanted to take part in it. Maybe he thought I wasn't ready for the task at hand because of my attitude.

Whatever his reasoning, as I looked at that list, I realized that, ultimately, the person who suffered the most from my snarky comments was me. From that moment on, my behaviour changed. I kept most of my smart-ass comments to myself. I realized how easy it was to make nasty comments from the safety of the sidelines. It's much harder to actually be in the game, taking the direct hit of the defeats and earning the successes as they come. Today, I have so much appreciation for people who take action and make things happen despite the snarky remarks that might be directed their way. I strive to be the person who assumes accountability and takes action, not the person who takes the easy road, issuing commentary from the sidelines.

There were other moments of growth during my time in the army. Early on in my service during a youth instructor course that I managed to wrangle my way into, I experienced a moment of freedom and true oneness. It was the first time I had to present to a group of my peers. There were fifty of us young soldiers altogether. Standing up in front of a group of that size represented my biggest fear come to fruition. Throughout my youth, I had managed to get myself out of these types of scenarios through any means possible: becoming violently ill, having an asthma attack, or whatever it took.

But this time, there was no way out.

All I had to do in this presentation was summarize the news of the week for my peers. Nonetheless, I was terrified and sweaty, and my heart started beating faster the moment I found out about this assignment. I also knew there was no way to get out of it. I understood that my future would involve standing up in front of people and instructing. This presentation would be my first taste of that, so I had to get over this horrible, very physical fear once and for all.

Leading up to this initial presentation, I took notes upon notes upon notes. I stayed away from my peers for the entire day as I attempted to prepare myself. The presentation was scheduled for five o'clock in the evening. As the time approached, I thought I was going to die.

The moment of truth finally arrived, and I stood up in front of the group, somewhat shaky and very sweaty. I lifted my copious notes so that I could read them. I started reading, keeping my eyes on the paper, acutely aware of my own frozen posture.

And then...something happened.

I felt all those eyes looking up at me, and it was almost as if I experienced a boost. Without thinking, I tossed the papers I had been holding into the air. The crowd didn't expect that, and they started laughing. That laughter gave me even more energy, which coursed through me as I spent the next ten minutes summarizing the events of the week. After the presentation ended, I felt a sense of elation surge through me. It was almost as if I were floating.

In that moment, I discovered a couple of things about myself that have stayed with me ever since. To my surprise, I learned that I thrive when presenting to or serving people. Until that experience, any interaction with another person (let alone a *group* of people) had caused me stress. I felt uncomfortably self-aware and, in turn, didn't behave naturally.

I realized that when I was presenting in a format like this, I could control my interactions with others. I could control when and if they spoke. I discovered that I was innately drawn to positions and scenarios that gave me control of the interactions. I realized that I had a history of doing this, although I hadn't been aware of it up to this point. At the deli, for instance, I had at first worked as a dishwasher, but before long, I started serving people at the front counter. I controlled those interactions by asking people how I could help them or opening with a joke or observation that controlled the tone of our interaction. The person I was serving might smile, laugh, or feel special. I felt great because I made them feel good.

To me, this was the opposite of mingling, a scenario in which I had never thrived—and still don't. My idea of a nightmare is standing in a room with people who have drinks in their hands and are searching for topics of conversation to engage in with strangers, repeating the same questions and answers over and over again until they find someone to get into a flow with. To this day, social mingling feels like a form of torture to me. Even as a middle-aged adult, I feel a knot form at the pit of my stomach. My body rises to an uncomfortable temperature, and I break out into a sweat when I enter a room filled with strangers. I'm always grateful that these types of events tend to take place in air-conditioned rooms.

That presentation also showed me that rewards come when we challenge our comfort level. For that reason, I have learned to force myself to join events that involve mingling with groups of strangers. I still don't love it, but I understand that these personal challenges generally pay off and help me grow in the long run.

That was certainly true in the case of my three years in the army.

CHAPTER FOUR

Finding My Path

I finished up my time in the army and returned to Canada when I was twenty-one. That marked the beginning of an in-between time.

As I got on the airplane and took my seat to return to Toronto, I felt somewhat emotional. I was leaving three years of army service in Israel, yet it didn't feel like home. My parents were in Toronto, and that didn't feel like home either. With no money or concrete plans for the future, I felt uprooted. Still, as the plane took off, I felt a great weight lift from my shoulders. It was one of those moments in life when you know everything will be okay in the long run, even if it feels uncertain in the moment.

When I got back to Toronto, I returned to work at Coleman's as I had as a teen, only this time I delivered catering orders. I didn't make a ton of money there, so I lived with my parents until I decided what to do next. I was planning on going to university, as I believed I was expected to, but I had no direction aside from that.

For a while, I wanted to become a civil engineer. I wanted to build houses and buildings like my British grandfather had. I always liked real estate and wanted to be a real estate mogul. Whenever I looked at a building, I found myself wondering what existed behind its walls, what kind of lives were being lived there. Urban living excited me. I thought of the city as a work of art, especially when looking at it from a distance. I thought that I would like to be a part of creating that. I did some investigating and realized that I was missing a high school chemistry credit that was required to apply to a civil engineering program. My high school grades weren't bad, but they were definitely not stellar. I figured that if I went to night school and got a decent mark in chemistry, I could get into a lesser-known university, and that was good enough for me.

When I registered for night school, I was both excited and nervous. I would be taking grade-thirteen chemistry. When I was in high school, I had taken grade-twelve chemistry, and as I recalled, it hadn't been that difficult. I figured this class wouldn't be too bad, considering it was the only one I was taking.

On the first night of class, I pulled my parents' car into the parking lot at the high school, thinking how great it would have been if I'd had my own car in high school and had been one of the cool students. I made my way to the old, boxy, brown structure, wondering what they had been thinking when they built it back in the sixties. How was this ugly structure expected to encourage students to learn? I made my way through the dreary corridor, trying to figure out where the chemistry class was. I entered the classroom and made my way to the back, where I sat down. Since I was a little early, I watched the other students walk in. They were a mix of high school kids and a handful of older students there to improve their grades or make up for a failed class. The teacher walked in soon after. All I remember about him is that he was grey: grey clothing and grey energy. He was far from excited to be there. When he opened his book and began the class, I sat up straight in my chair and listened intently. As the class went on, I shrunk down lower and lower. It was as if the teacher were speaking a foreign language. It seemed that I had forgotten everything I had once known about chemistry over the course of the past three years. Terror crept into my heart. Had I forgotten how to study? Was that skill gone forever?

By the time the class ended, I was terrified. There was no way I was going to get through this class, let alone get a good grade. I decided to read up before the second class and give it another chance. Two classes later, I understood that my memory had erased all chemistry-related language and information. I guess my brain cells were occupied with how to get through the army rather than retaining the names of chemical elements. I dropped the night class and found myself back at square one. *Who am I?* I wondered. *What am I going to be?* These were stressful questions.

As I looked through the university courses, waiting for something to jump out at me, I found myself drawn to a hospitality and hotel management degree at a university located in downtown Toronto. It took me back to the fancy hotel in Tel Aviv where my father's business had been located. As a kid, I'd always looked forward to going there. It felt so exotic, like being in a different country. *I could do this,* I thought. I decided to register for that program at Ryerson University. It couldn't have been more different from civil engineering, but I had all the required credits and would get to spend more time in hotels. That didn't sound so bad. Plus, it felt like a relief to have the decision made.

I was very nervous at the beginning of university. My spoken English was good, so my writing skills should have been acceptable—but they weren't. I couldn't put a paragraph together without misspelling most of the words, not to mention my abysmal grammar. In addition, I didn't know how to type on a computer. I had no clue how I would write an exam, let alone an essay.

During the first week at university, I met a really nice guy named Justin. He was born into a very wealthy family (his father was one of the city's top lawyers) and raised in Toronto. Justin had graduated from one of Canada's top private high schools and had a degree in English from another university. He definitely knew his shit. I think we connected because we were both a little older than the eighteen-year-olds attending their first year of uni.

The second week of school, we were sitting next to each other when the professor handed out an assignment. It wasn't anything crazy: a ten-page, double-spaced essay due in two weeks. But when I heard the assignment, I got a knot in my stomach, and terror washed over me. I just knew I was going to be discovered as a fraud, and everyone would find out that a kid in grade two could write better than me. Thankfully, the professor proceeded to tell us that the assignment was to be done in pairs. I immediately turned to Justin before anyone else had the chance. Smiling to cover my fear, I asked him if he wanted to partner up. He nodded. *Crisis averted*, I thought. I would go to the library to do the research and put in the work, and Justin could take care of the typing and make sure the project was well written.

The two of us decided to meet later in the day to discuss the project. Justin was so cool about the whole thing. "No worries," he said. "This is an easy one. I can write it in a couple of hours."

The next day, I picked Justin up to come back to my derelict apartment. On the way, he asked me to stop by a drug store. Just before he got out of the car, Justin asked if he could borrow ten bucks. "Of course you can," I replied. This happened a couple more times during the two weeks we worked on the project together. Over that time, we discussed the project and devised a strategy, but not one word was typed on the computer. I was getting worried, but Justin kept promising that it was a piece of cake.

The evening before the project was due, I drove my mom's old Honda to the rich part of town to meet at Justin at his place. I'd be lying if I said I wasn't worried by that point.

The sun was setting as I turned right onto his street, which was lined with big, old maple trees and beautiful houses. I thought how lucky Justin was to live there. I'd never even *visited* this neighbourhood before.

When I arrived at Justin's, I was so focussed on getting the right number that, at first, I didn't even pay attention to the house itself. It wasn't until I got out of my car that I realized it was the biggest house on this street of big houses. I rang the bell nervously, wondering if I really had the right place. As I was thinking about how much I didn't belong there, a man in his early thirties opened the door. He looked at me. His eyes glanced back towards my old Honda and then back at me again.

"Can I help you?"

"Is this Justin's home?" I asked nervously.

He stared at me for a couple of seconds before nodding and gesturing me into the massive house. I could see the pool through the distant back door. I looked around and saw a staircase. I instinctively turned towards it, expecting Justin to come down the stairs. The guy cleared his throat and nodded his head ever so slightly towards another staircase in the opposite direction. They had two staircases! I heard Justin calling me.

It turned out that Justin had an apartment bigger than mine within this massive house. We sat down in his living room. I was anxious for Justin to translate all my legwork to words on paper. But he was acting weird and unfocussed. He kept going to the washroom, and his normally pale skin was red. Just as he had for the past two weeks, Justin kept assuring me that he could type up our paper in no time—but time was running out! Finally, around eleven that night, he typed the opening paragraph. We were sitting next to each other on the sofa when his body gave, and he collapsed on me.

I jumped up in surprise. "Justin, are you okay? What's going on?"

He struggled to pull himself up, and then the truth came out. "Alon, I'm sorry. I'm completely wasted."

Turns out Justin had been an alcoholic since he was a teenager. He was sent to boarding school because his parents had no time for him. They were always either at work or travelling. All the cabinets in the house had locks on them because he stole stuff to get money to buy booze. He was given exact change for subway trips. The guy who had opened the door was there to keep an eye on Justin when he was home. Before coming to university, Justin had just completed three months at a fancy rehab facility in the US. It turned out that the money Justin had borrowed from me was used to buy over-the-counter medicine that contained alcohol, which he proceeded to hide in his toilet tank.

As Justin was telling me all this, I felt a double blow. The first blow came from feeling so sorry for him. It was clear that he was a really nice guy with severe issues. The other blow came from the fact that I now didn't have an essay to hand in the following day.

The next day, I worked up my best puppy-dog eyes— not that I needed to try too hard. I was both depressed and terrified. Thankfully, my professor agreed that I could hand it in one day late without a penalty. When I got back to my apartment that afternoon, I sat in front of the computer and began typing the first essay I'd ever written, using just my index finger. An hour later, I had written just a paragraph.

Just then, my mom happened to stop by to see how I was doing. I guess she saw the despair in my eyes because she sat down next to me and made me one of the kindest offers I've ever received. "Let's do this together, Alon," she said. My mom was not an academic. She read many books, but she had told me that school was a negative experience for her.

Despite the fact that I'd never seen her type anything in my life, my mom gently nudged me away from the computer and said, "Okay, you tell me what to write, and I'll type." I was so happy in that moment to know that I wasn't alone in this. I sat on the bed, and since I had already done all the research, I was able to formulate the content of the essay. My mom wasn't a good typist either, but we made progress. After a couple of hours, I even began typing. I was still slow, but now I had momentum. Together, we finished the essay around one in the morning. I'll never forget how thankful I was for my mom that day. I sometimes wonder if I would have quit university had she not shown up at the precise moment she did. Did her coincidental appearance and willingness to help change the course of my life? One thing is for sure: Mom saved the day!

I handed in the essay the next day. I knew it was far from perfect, but I was proud to have finished. A week later I got it back with a B-minus. I was so happy! I immediately took the essay to show my mom. Even as I write this story, I have tears in my eyes and a big lump in my throat thinking back on that moment.

The previous summer, shortly after I'd returned to Canada from Israel, I had met a woman named Michelle. She was the daughter of friends who lived in Israel and had come to Canada with her mom to visit relatives. Michelle and I formed a friendship and spent some time together as I showed her around the city. When summer drew to a close, Michelle went back to Israel while I started university. After I finished up that first year, I decided to go back to Israel for the summer. Michelle and I reconnected during that visit and fell in love. A year later, she moved to Toronto, and we decided to get married. I attended my third year of university as Michelle mastered making rice with my father and served Jewish Orthodox couples and families sweet-and-sour chicken balls.

The two of us went out with my university friends, and I partied hard at the time. By "partied hard," I mean that I drank way more than my body could handle. I think I was known as "the puker." My friends welcomed Michelle's arrival because she took over the task of making sure I hit the toilet when I threw up.

Life started to move quickly, taking on the momentum that often comes with adulthood. I graduated from university a little less than two years after Michelle and I got married. I was twenty-six and focussed on opening my own business. During my fourth year at university, my friend Harry and I had written up a business plan for a healthy pita-bread sandwich shop. Well, I did most of the work, but Harry pitched in by putting together a few easy financial tables. The idea was to make a different variety of fresh pita every day, each with healthy Middle Eastern fillings. Kind of like the Middle Eastern version of Subway.

Harry and I got an A on that project. It was one of the only A's I ever got in all the years I spent in school. To this day, I continue to remind Harry that I was responsible for getting him that A. He may have a different recollection of events, but that is not important.

But the good grade was only the beginning. As part of the project, all the business plans submitted in that class were evaluated by a guest panel. Ours took first place, and we won three hundred dollars. Harry and I decided to invest that prize money into a long session at a local pub that very night.

Perhaps you're wondering why I had such a specific idea for this business plan. I learned how to make pita bread with my Jewish-Yemeni grandmother and aunt, who never bought bread from the store. In our family, the women made fresh bread *every day*, and every meal included fresh pita bread.

I always loved the smell of fresh dough. I loved touching it to see how sticky it was; when it was extra sticky, parts of the dough would stick to my finger, which meant I could lick it and chew the raw dough. My aunt always told me to stop doing that because it was unhealthy for my stomach, but I wasn't deterred.

Once she finished kneading the dough, she put it in a bowl, covered it with a towel, and put it in a warm place to rise. I took a peek every once in a while to see how the dough was coming along and marvel at the bubbles that formed in it, as if the dough was alive. I found the smell of the fermenting yeast intoxicating as it wafted out from under the towel.

Once the dough had risen, my aunt scooped it out with her strong hands and kneaded it one more time before breaking it up into smaller balls, which she covered with a thin layer of flour so they wouldn't stick to the tray. She placed them in rows with enough distance between them to allow them to expand. Soon after, she turned the range on and warmed up the little modern pita oven. When the dough balls puffed up, my aunt lifted the towel and ever so delicately touched one dough ball to see if it bounced back in a very specific way. When it did, she hand-stretched the dough, placed it on the piping-hot range, and covered it with a special lid covered with red-hot coils. I remained near the pan, peeking through a small hole in it to watch as the dough was placed between the immense heat coming from both the top and bottom of the pan. Within seconds, the pita began puffing up, as if by magic.

The beautiful smell of fresh bread made its way through the apartment, and slowly but surely, the men who were sitting in the living room talking and cracking sunflower seeds made their way into the kitchen. The first pitas never made it to the table. Despite the fact that they were still piping hot, they were ripped apart by a host of hands clamoring for a piece of the fresh bread. My aunt pretended to get angry with the men for interfering with the baking process, but I could tell that she secretly loved the praise and attention.

When I was sixteen, I bought my own pita-making pan and began experimenting. I loved baking, and I also loved the human interaction that took place around the food, not to mention the compliments and attention from the people who ate my bread.

When I was done with university, I gave the business plan I had created to my father to review. He got very excited about it and proposed that we make the business happen together. I quickly agreed to his proposal. My dad was sixty years old at the time, and my parents were not wealthy. I was an out-of-work recent graduate with $25,000 in student loans. My parents were willing to sell their only investment property, which left them with $50,000 after paying off the mortgage. I was nervous about the risk they were taking on this business, but I was willing to go ahead with it anyway.

We found a bank that was willing to give us a $100,000 small-business loan as long as we invested that $50,000 as well. I will never forget the evening my father delivered the loan documents to me to sign. I was twenty-six years old and felt the responsibility of my parents' retirement on my narrow, inexperienced shoulders. I knew that once I signed the pile of documents on my dining room table, there was no turning back. I would be responsible for paying back the $100,000 and making sure that my parents were cared for financially. *Fuck it*, I thought. *I have nothing now anyway, so I might as well go for it!*

With the loan in hand, my father and I opened our store in a not-so-good neighbourhood. I remember standing outside the store as we were renovating it, counting the number of people who walked by on the very busy street. I figured all we needed was 1 percent of those pedestrians to walk through our door, and we would be rich! However, once we opened the doors to release the wonderful smell of fresh bread, very few people walked in. In fact, that first week, only the nosy neighbours who occupied the other storefronts in the area came in to check us out. I got very worried and felt fear overtake me. This business had cost my parents their pension; I had to make it work!

Thankfully, pressure pushed me into action. I printed a bunch of buy-one-get-one-free coupons and walked two blocks east to the big government offices, determined to find customers there. I walked from one floor to another, offering samples, smiles, and coupons. I was chased out by security guards more than once. For some reason, they seemed to assume I was starting out at the floor level, so I quickly figured out that the best way to give out coupons and samples out was to start at the top floor and work my way down.

Almost immediately, a line began to form at the store. Everyone figured we were kicking ass, but we still had plenty of lessons to learn. We didn't charge enough for our freshly made sandwiches, and we gave our customers way too many options. All of this came from a good place: we wanted to have happy customers.

One week after opening, my wife, Michelle, quit her job as a waitress and joined my dad and me at the store. The three of us and a couple of part-time employees carried the load. At first, I worked the cash register, but within just a few days of joining us, Michelle took me off the register because I was giving away too many items. It was the right call; it turns out I wasn't good at taking money from people, as much as I wanted to succeed.

Four years after we opened, my brother, Guy, joined my dad and me in the business. He invested some much-needed cash so that we could evolve our small restaurant into a wholesale bakery. We specialized in healthy flatbreads and crackers, which we sold to stores throughout Toronto. At that point, our dad took a back seat, and Guy and I spearheaded the company's growth from there.

Other things were changing quickly too. Two years after opening the store, Michelle and I welcomed our first son. Within a period of four years, we had three kids—two sons and a daughter. Both of us were fully devoted to the business and the family, and life took on a velocity of its own.

CHAPTER FIVE

Energy

In those early years of our marriage, Michelle and I lived in downtown Toronto, within walking distance of everything. I spent lots of time walking while listening to music and found that it became a very meditative experience. As I walked, my thoughts wandered until sometimes they vanished altogether. I was able to detach my mind and drift into a state of dreamy observation—as if I were watching a movie of a streetscape merging fluidly together with all the other people, dogs, and cars.

One afternoon, I headed out to the gym. It was a twenty-minute walk towards the downtown core. As I walked, I felt the usual dreamy kind of flow of being in the zone, and then, suddenly, I started feeling odd. The sensation began as a tingle in my stomach that quickly grew to become a powerful ball of energy that radiated throughout my body. It felt like nothing I had ever experienced before—as if a light switch was flipped on. But instead of casting a sharp, direct light, it was as if warm and wavy rays of light were flowing through me. On one hand, it was an entirely new experience. But on the other hand, it felt very familiar.

The sensation took me by surprise and also scared me a little.

A quick conversation ensued in my head. One side of my brain wanted to stop this immediately. It was too scary and powerful. But almost instantly, the other side of my brain let me know that everything was okay, and I could stop this experience at any time if I wanted to. I instantly knew this second voice was correct, so I decided to let the experience run its course.

I moved over to the side of the pavement and allowed my eyes to close. Once I did that, the energy ball became so much stronger. It seemed as if the entire sun was condensed into a tiny ball, emanating energy out of my stomach. Tears began to flow from my eyes, and I felt a love that extended out to touch everything known and unknown, every rock and every being that exists. All of it. I can only imagine what people must have thought of me as I stood there on the sidewalk with my eyes shut and tears running down my face. Maybe they thought a new drug had hit the streets of Toronto.

I have no idea how long this experience lasted because I lost myself in it. Eventually, the feeling subsided, and the ball of energy dissipated. I slowly opened my eyes and lifted my arm to wipe the streaks of fresh tears from my face, and my heartbeat and breath both made their way back to their regular pace.

I couldn't ignore that experience—it felt too big and too real. I began searching for courses and teachers that could shed light on what had happened. I read esoteric books about energy, yoga, healing, reiki, and anything else that felt like it might be related or could provide an explanation for what had happened to me. Oddly enough, a very good friend of mine connected with me a week after the incident and told me about an amazing Russian healer who had helped his mother. As it turned out, this healer was starting a bioenergy course the following week. There was one catch, though: the course was in Russian.

I didn't care. I couldn't sign up quickly enough—despite the fact that I don't speak a word of Russian.

The course took place in an office space located in an industrial park north of the city. I had no idea what to expect even as I parked my car and walked to the front door of the building. There were so many unknowns: the healer himself, what bioenergy even *was*—oh, and, of course,

Russian. As I entered the room, I saw a middle-aged guy with long hair and piercing eyes sitting there, with no emotion evident on his face. About twelve chairs had been organized into three rows facing him. Half of the chairs were occupied by middle-aged Russian women who were looking at the healer as if they were trying to figure him out. Every once in a while, one of the women whispered to another.

In situations like this, I usually pick a chair in the back. I've learned that position keeps me out of the full view of the presenter and offers me an easy escape route. But this time, against my instincts, my feet walked me right up to a seat in the front of the room, directly across from the healer. As I sat down, I realized what I had just done, but it was too late to escape. I accepted the fact that I would remain right here, no matter what, until the evening drew to an end. Oddly, I didn't feel as stressed out about this as I normally would have. I glanced at the healer, trying not to look too interested, and noticed that his eyes were blank. Usually, when I look into a person's eyes, I can very quickly decide if I like them or not, but this time there was nothing.

As it turned out, my friend and I were the only men in the group. I've often wondered what about new and esoteric experiences attract more women than men. Are women more open to risk and learning about the extraordinary? Do men's egos prevent them from putting themselves in unknown, vulnerable, "unmanly" situations where they might be forced to confront something about themselves? Or is it the risk of becoming emotional in front of a group that keeps many men from courses like this?

The healer started speaking—of course, in Russian. My friend translated until I told him it wasn't necessary. I would figure it out. We were told to close our eyes, uncross our legs, and place our hands on our thighs. I glanced around the room to make sure I had assumed the correct position. I closed my eyes for a few seconds but couldn't resist opening them a crack to see what the instructor was doing. His eyes were shut and his arms were raised, with his palms pointed towards us. It seemed as if he was in another world. I shut my eyes once again, and within seconds, I felt a gentle tingle along my arms. Slowly, the strange sensation grew stronger. It was as if an army of ants was crawling all over my arms. I don't know how much time passed before the healer told us to open our eyes when we felt ready (which I knew thanks to my friend's translation).

This experience opened my eyes to a new world. I continued seeing the healer after the initial course and learned a whole lot more about energy and bioenergy. As I learned more, I tried to help people in need by sending energy their way. Every time I did, I found that I had no energy the following day. Over time, I've learned that it's unhealthy for me to give my own energy to fix someone else. We need to use our own energy to heal. What I—and we *all*—can do for others who are struggling is be there and lend a hand. Each of our journeys is our own to create.

I came to realize that energy is a very real thing in humans and in animals.

While I was delving into energy, I was also working at our store. One day, I was dumping the old fryer oil into a big drum located in the parking lot behind our restaurant to be picked up by a company that removed the used oil for free. The oil was dark and somewhat rancid. As I sat on the back stairs, taking some time alone to restore my energy following a busy lunch rush, the oil truck began reversing towards our building. The beeping of the truck as it moved backward pierced my ears and seemed to go on forever. At last, the truck stopped, and with it, so did the annoying noise. The truck driver jumped out and made his way to the overflowing oil drum. I got up and introduced myself.

"I have a question for you," I said.

"Sure," he replied.

"What do you guys use the burned oil for?" I assumed that it might be passed along to the cosmetics industry, perhaps to make soap. Although if that was the case, I wanted to know how they got rid of the horrible smell and burned grime in the oil.

He asked, "Do you really want to know?"

"Yes! Why wouldn't I?"

He paused for a second before replying. "They use it in chicken feed."

"You must be joking!"

"No, I'm not. That's why this service is free."

I was grossed out just thinking about this. I pictured chickens plucking this gross oil out of feeding containers, the black oil dripping down their beaks.

About two weeks after that incident, I was speaking with my brother on the phone, and he told me that he had become a vegetarian a while back. At that moment, I realized that I hadn't touched any meat since that oil pickup. At that moment, I decided to become a full-blown vegetarian.

Ten years later, I realized that even though I ate healthily, I was constantly sick. Every cold that visited our city made a pit stop in my body. I was frustrated with being weak and sickly. One day, I happened to read a book about blood types. It explained that people with blood type O need to consume meat. For some reason, that resonated with me. A few days later, I began eating meat again, and I felt much better. But in order for me to go back to being a carnivore, I had to accept the fact that I was responsible for killing the animal I was eating. With that realization, the way in which animals are raised and treated became very important to me. I was responsible for the death of the animal, and I was *also* responsible for its well-being while it was alive.

Today, before I eat meat, I take a few seconds to recognize that I am consuming a living creature. I thank that animal for its sacrifice and only then do I proceed to eat it.

CHAPTER SIX

Choking in the Suburbs

Life in our little apartment downtown was great for Michelle and me. We enjoyed all our little city routines, and better yet, we never had to drive anywhere. On Tuesdays, we went to the movies in the evening. On Wednesdays, we always had half-price nachos with a bunch of friends at our favourite Mexican restaurant. Every Wednesday, we immediately spent the money we had saved on nachos on pints of beer. We spent Saturday mornings at the coffee shop where all the dog owners met before going on their morning walk. Mind you, Michelle and I didn't have a dog; I was there for the fresh blueberry muffins laden with chocolate. After our morning muffin, we would often have Indian food at our favourite curry joint. And any day of the week, you might find us at our favourite cheap Thai restaurant, right around the corner from our apartment. These routines gave us a sense of home.

Even though we lived in the centre of the city, the actual street we lived on was green and very quiet. Most people perceive the downtown area of Toronto as noisy and dirty. That's true of the main arteries, but in reality, downtown Toronto has plenty of quiet green spaces that are very walkable.

When Michelle was pregnant with our first son, we started talking about moving out of our cozy downtown apartment. Michelle wanted to move to the suburbs for our son (and any kids we might have in the future). I understood her rationale. The apartment we lived in was perfect for two people, but it wasn't made for a family. We also wanted to try to buy a place of our own rather than continuing to rent, and we couldn't afford anything downtown.

In the end, we found a small house we could afford that wasn't too far from the new commercial bakery and was conveniently located behind our favourite bagel place. Michelle and I and our new son spent a couple of years there before moving farther away from the city. It was as if we couldn't make that jump directly to the suburbs without some titration first. The purchase of our first house allowed us to upgrade to our next home, which was farther north. There, we had our second son. That house was very practical. It had four bedrooms, a full basement, and no soul. It was identical to all the other houses in that neighbourhood. It was located on a cul-de-sac, which was good for the kids to play on and the parents to chat with one another about whatever people in the suburbs talk about.

After two years of living in the copy-paste house and the birth of our daughter, a friend mentioned that there was a house for sale that I just had to see. The first time I saw our next home in the far suburbs, I immediately fell in love. I clearly remember standing at the gate and looking into the massive backyard that included a swimming pool overhung by huge, old trees. *I could live here. This place could inspire me*, I thought. *I'll make an offer.* My next thought was, *How can I sell this to Michelle?* She loves to cook, so I promised her a brand-new, modern kitchen. After seeing the house with her a couple of times and selling the positive impact the backyard would have on the kids (and, of course, frequently mentioning that new kitchen), she agreed, and we made an offer and moved in a couple of months later. Bye-bye copy-paste suburban home, hello boring and not-so-quiet green suburb.

All five of us were very excited to move in. At the time, it didn't feel like we were giving up *so* much by moving even farther away from the city. Michelle and I figured we wouldn't have any use for the park we used to frequent because we could just use the pool all the time and play in the yard instead. By the second summer, we rarely used the pool, which was a pain to maintain. The massive lawn meant that I spent my weekends pushing a noisy, smelly lawn mower around. I quickly came to feel like a slave to our home. And when I finally got to sit down on the back porch on the weekends, there was rarely a quiet moment. All weekend, every weekend, at any given moment, at least one of our neighbours was using their own loud machine to maintain their own massive yard. If I wanted to get some peace, I had to go inside to get it.

So there we were in the suburbs. The place where our kids could run outside and play and where my soul was crushed. I fell into the role of dad in the suburbs because that's what I was supposed to do. I took the kids to their play dates, and as they played, I withered away the hours carrying on empty, soul-crushing conversations with the other parents. After all, that's how it works. As the kids venture out into the world and go to daycare and then school, the parents of their friends become your friends.

Before you know it, you're getting invited to all these get-togethers where the conversations mostly revolve around the weather, luxury cars, and home square footage. Then, on the rare occasion when you're not in the suburbs, you find yourself visiting those same people in their big, beautiful cottages on the lake. There, you talk about the same things you talk about every other time: houses, cars, careers, and how talented the kids are.

I found that the people who talked the most in the suburbs were usually the ones who were the most successful. It's funny how the people who have the most money also seem to have the most influence over communal wisdom. I found that when this type of person did stop talking about themselves for long enough to ask me a question, it was usually nothing more than a setup for them to change the topic of the conversation and continue talking about themselves. I was pained by these conversations I constantly found myself in. My social life was like being in a continuous state of needing to vomit as I listened to our new "friends," who I considered to be boring, self-absorbed people.

I can't even imagine how people who were struggling financially felt in this environment. Michelle and I did okay, but I still found myself stressed out by everything we *didn't* have compared to everyone else. It was impossible not to compare myself to others in our community, even though our family was somewhere in the middle financially.

The volume of the voices in my head increased. I didn't feel like I belonged to this group. I didn't *want* to be part of this group. It was as if I was playing a part in a play, and the mental cost of playing that role increased as each day went by.

We used to spend quite a bit of time with Michelle's best friend and her husband. Part of the unwritten rules of that relationship—and so many others in the suburbs, in my experience—is that our kids, who went to the same daycare, spent time together too. The husband was smart and financially successful, and his wife was pretty and very warm. But whenever we spent time with them, the husband always put his wife down. Eventually, he didn't even need to put her down anymore because she did it herself. Being with them was painful. He was one of those people who always needed to control the room. He set the tone of the conversation, and whenever he wanted something, his wife jumped up to get it for him. Not once did I hear him thank her for anything. The dynamic seemed to be that it was her role to quietly agree with him. His idea of conversation was a monologue. Being with them not only felt like a waste of time but was also mentally depleting.

One of the happiest days of my life was when I forgot to invite this guy to a family event we were hosting. Well, I didn't so much forget to invite him as I never considered inviting him in the first place. He was so insulted by this omission that he decided to sever our "friendship." I heard through the grapevine that he thought we were close enough that I was obligated to invite him to our family events. At first he cut me out of his life, which was welcome news for me. Not long after, his wife, Michelle's best friend at the time, began finding excuses to distance herself from Michelle. I'm sure the controlling husband had something to do with that. Life got a little better for me at that point.

Thinking back on those years, I'm surprised how many couples had dynamics like this. To me, being in that type of relationship would have been equivalent to a lifetime of psychological imprisonment with hard labour.

While living in the suburbs, stress built up inside me. Not only was living in that type of environment hard for me, but going to work became difficult too. During those years, everything got hard. Not being in my element affected every aspect of my life, including work. Even though I liked marketing and product development, there was always an invisible cloud over my head. It was as if I was on autopilot. I didn't get excited by anything.

I sat in our boardroom during meetings, distracted by thoughts of how much I hated everything and how much I didn't want to be there. I would reach the end of a meeting only to realize that I hadn't absorbed anything because I was so distracted by being miserable.

Friday afternoons stand out as being particularly awful. On my way home from work every week, I stopped at a strip mall to buy stuff. Under the pretense of shopping, I really used the stop as an opportunity to sit in the car and breathe while I gathered the strength to go home. Those moments when it was just me and the quiet were so dear to me. I wanted quiet, and there was just so little of it.

For as distracted and miserable as I was, it turned out that I was also very good at disguising my feelings. No one knew where I was at emotionally, including Michelle, who I saw every day, cared for, and loved. But I also slowly began to dislike her during this period. The invisible steam was building in me, and with that, so was my anger towards Michelle.

As I was coming to learn, the suburbs were more than just a place—at least to me. They were also a mindset—an energy that was killing my individuality. People belonged to herds. Every family had their group, but I didn't have a group. I didn't belong. With time, I came to learn that I did not fit in the suburbs, either physically or socially.

One Christmas, Michelle and I decided to take the family out of town. A wealthy friend suggested that we use a high-end travel agency to book a trip to Costa Rica. The agency took care of everything. Upon arriving in San Jose, our family was greeted by one of those limo drivers holding up a sheet of paper with our last name on it. This was a first for me. I had always been envious of those important-looking travelers before, and now, here we were!

The next day, a fancy Jeep that could hold all five of us and our stuff was delivered directly to our hotel. From there, we travelled through the beautiful Costa Rican landscape all the way up to the northwest corner of the country.

I had always heard great things about Costa Rica. Mostly, I had heard how great the locals were and that it was a true gathering place where it was possible to meet other interesting people from all over the world. I was ready for this experience, but it didn't happen. Most of the designer-jean-clad, middle-age or older guests at our five-star hotel kept to themselves. At first, I thought that maybe it was us. Maybe everyone else was hanging out in a secret common room, having drinks and laughing together, and we just hadn't been invited. After a few days, though, I realized there was no secret room; everyone was just keeping to themselves.

Don't get me wrong. Costa Rica was beautiful, and we had a good time as a family. But that's really all I have to say about that trip. It doesn't stand out in any other way. The five-star hotel was nice, but I don't remember it all these years later.

The following year, we wanted to travel for Christmas again, but this time we were short on cash, as most entrepreneurs periodically are. At the last minute, we found a super cheap, all-inclusive deal on a trip for five to Cuba. It cost one-fifth of what we'd paid to go to Costa Rica the year before. We decided to take advantage of the opportunity to get some sun.

The first thing I noticed was how friendly and chatty everyone was on the bus from the airport to the hotel where we were staying. The tourists at this resort clearly came from working- to middle-class families. We got to know a couple of dairy farmers who had just retired and were enjoying one of their first trips ever because it had been so difficult for them to take time off before this point. We talked to a hairdresser who was also from Toronto. We met people of all different stripes, from all different walks of life. It was evident that the travellers we came across in Cuba were genuinely excited about the adventure at hand, and they were happy to share their excitement with others. That week was so much fun, and it still stands out in my mind all these years later.

The contrast between these two vacations was so stark. It made me wonder if people changed when they had more money, more stuff, and more experiences. Why was everyone in Costa Rica so much more closed off than the people we met in Cuba? It wasn't lost on me that my family had also been more closed off in Costa Rica, when we travelled alone in a car and stayed in plush accommodations that didn't require us to leave the hotel grounds. The truth of the matter was that there wasn't much of an opportunity to mingle with others.

I started to wonder if there was something about wealth that caused humans to build walls around themselves and their possessions. I started to wonder about how trust seems to diminish as wealth rises, and it struck me as funny and ironic that the wealthy would become distrustful of strangers. Because here's the thing: eventually, the ones closest to you will assume your money and possessions— not the strangers.

CHAPTER SEVEN

Escaping the Suburbs

Aside from our family vacations, I made a point of getting away as much as I could on my own. Every year, these getaways became a little more frequent until it got to the point where I was in a constant quest to escape my own life. The suburbs and family life felt more and more like jail to me as each year went by, and I began developing various coping mechanisms to escape the reality of my home, my work, and myself.

By then, the bakery was selling our products across North America, which was great for me because it meant business travel was a part of life. I had to go to food shows, meetings, and presentations. My travel volume increased in direct relation to my feelings of being trapped and my level of emotional and mental pain. Very quickly, my entire family got used to this schedule. Michelle didn't mind staying with the kids, and they all had their routines and seemed to be happy. At least, that was the story I told myself.

Being home caused me anxiety. Family life stressed me out, even though I loved the kids and respected Michelle.

Each time I rolled my carry-on out the front door and headed to the airport, I felt a sense of freedom wash over me. It was as if something lifted inside of me. Even though I knew it was just temporary relief, it was good enough.

As I walked into the airport, the pressure lifted even more. The smell of the terminal and the energy of the people moving all around me felt so good. I even created an airport ritual. Each time I arrived, I bought a copy of *The Economist* and a couple of bars of chocolate, which kept me happily occupied on the airplane. When the plane took off, it felt as if all my troubles stayed on the ground below. As I flew over massive expanses of land, looking down at the cities and villages below, I wondered if God looked down like this from above, marvelling at how all of us stressed-out humans had gotten ourselves into this state. I wanted that feeling I felt while flying—that sense of distance from reality—to stay with me when I got home. It didn't.

I got another high when I checked in to the hotel and then walked to my room, anxiously anticipating the moment when I could close the door behind me and be all alone.

It was the perfect scenario. To those at home, I was working. This meant that calls and messages could be ignored or forgotten. After all, the agreement that Michelle and I had made when our first son was born was that I would put all my energy into the business while she served as the main caregiver. Michelle's dream was to have a family, and she loved taking care of kids. I, on the other hand, was all in on growing the business, not to mention that my caregiving abilities were inferior to hers, as much as I tried. We understood this about each other, and it was part of our agreement. At least, that was what I kept telling myself.

A lot of my work trips were to food shows, which were composed of massive rows of booths, each representing a business that presented its latest product, positioning it as the next game-changer.

The energy at the food shows was a lot like high school—only this time, I liked it. Everyone attending was on vacation from their personal reality, and this sense of freedom created a buzz in the air.

It probably won't surprise you to hear that despite the fact that everyone was technically there for the event, it was evenings spent at the bars around the convention centre that everyone anticipated the most. I participated too, drinking excessively with my colleagues, although I didn't partake in the extracurricular activities some of them did. As the hour grew later and the alcohol released people's inhibitions to greater and greater degrees, the late-night texts and calls began. You can imagine what happened next. It was like camp for adults. We all got a break from our boring lives, away from our kids and spouses. Yes, we all went there to work during the day, but mentally, we were free—hundreds if not thousands of us.

Being in this environment gave me an escape from the external pressures of the life I had created in the suburbs. However, my inner demons were still lurking and growing. Each night, I ended up back in my room watching porn. My computer screen felt like the ticket to free my feelings. Once I snapped the screen shut, I buried my feelings away again, even deeper than before.

Even on the weekends I stayed home, I started going out by myself. I think that after a while, Michelle could see the pressure building up in me and knew that I needed some space. She has always been such a considerate person.

Every Sunday night, I headed out to a cool, old, dark diner that was open twenty-four hours a day. I sat in the same two-seater booth located directly under a dim light every time. The five-dollar pint of beer came first, followed by the room-temperature tuna melt. I ate with one hand and held a book down with the other. As I ate, I pondered how the tuna melt was never hot when it arrived at the table, yet the cheese was melted. Each time my order arrived, I wondered if today was the day the tuna melt would arrive hot, but it never did. I came to the conclusion that the staff was trained incredibly well. As I sat there pondering my tuna melt and drinking my couple of beers, the alcohol took its effect. Having been transported for a couple of hours, I left the diner feeling ready to return home and take on Monday morning. It was a safe place for me to decompress, detach from family life, and just be myself. It was an act of self-preservation, I suppose.

All of this worked...until it didn't.

As the pressure inside me continued to build, I found that I needed to escape more, and I began leaving the house on Saturday evenings too. I told myself that once the kids went to sleep, it was okay to go out. By this point, things were not good between Michelle and me, so she didn't seem to care if I took off.

My Saturday ritual was to head out and see Niki. I had met Niki a few years before, when I volunteered at an organization where more seasoned entrepreneurs mentored young entrepreneurs in the process of launching their business. I was matched as a mentor with Niki, who was importing organic olive oil from her family back in Crete. As time progressed, the two of us became good friends.

In addition to her import business, Niki also worked as a bartender at one of Toronto's busiest bars. She wasn't aware of my personal struggles, although in retrospect, I'm sure she had a question or two about why a married father like me had time to hang out at the bar where she worked every Saturday night. Later, I found out that Niki's girlfriend thought that I was interested in Niki. I can certainly see why she suspected that.

I suppose I sought out Niki's company because I really liked her as a friend. Also, I suspect that deep down, I knew that Niki probably wouldn't judge me. Every Saturday, I texted Niki to let her know that I was in the area. I never told her that I drove all the way downtown just to spend a little time with her as an escape from my own reality. Niki instructed me to tell the bouncer that I was her cousin so that he would let me in, despite the line of up to a hundred people waiting in the cold. Every time I approached the bouncer, I wondered if he was going to send me to the back of the line. He never did, though. I guess Niki was a big deal there.

Stepping through the doors of that bar felt like entering a different world. The loud thrum of the dance music pulsed all around me as I pushed my way through the intoxicated young dancers. Here came the forty-something suburban dad, looking to escape his life!

I always found Niki handling the back bar on her own, serving a multitude of outstretched hands, exchanging notes of money in return for drinks. Niki was so focussed on her work that it usually took her a couple of minutes to notice me leaning against the wall, off to the side of the bar. Niki barely had time to talk, but even so, she always took short breaks to exchange a few words with me.

Looking back, I'm so grateful to Niki for just going with it. Never once did she ask me what I was doing there. She didn't probe. She just accepted me. That was all I needed. I was there because I knew the cool bartender. I fit in. I was special. After a short time, I realized that I was in the way and took off. Yet another Saturday escape was a momentary success.

I drove home afterwards, hoping that everyone was asleep, and quietly made my way to my room in the basement, where I now slept. This move from the bedroom I shared with Michelle had happened gradually. I'm a light sleeper, and on top of that, my body emits inhuman amounts of heat as I sleep. Earlier on in our marriage, I used to shed the blanket and wait for the heat to dissipate. On the nights it was really bad, I quietly rolled out of bed to sleep in the basement, where it was eternally cold.

In the beginning, I spent the odd night sleeping in the basement for that legitimate reason. But after a while, it became an excuse. And then, over time, I realized that I just didn't want to be in bed with my wife. It didn't even feel like a decision; it was more like there was a physical force pushing me out of our shared bed. And so, over time, it became normal for me to sleep in the basement. We began seeing a therapist, and those sessions allowed us to run our lives as normally as possible—except for the fact that we didn't sleep together. Other than that, Michelle and I operated like a well-oiled machine, dealing with the day-to-day routine of family and work.

Of all my escapes, the one I considered to be the ultimate was my yearly trip to Maui, where my best friend from university, Harry, had moved with his wife and daughter. Initially, I thought Harry was crazy to move to Maui. He was a partner at a successful travel company that afforded him the chance to travel all over the world in luxury as a tour operator. When Harry told me that he was planning on moving, I didn't understand. His life seemed perfect from the outside. Why would he want to change it all? I told Harry as much, but he was determined to make the move. His reasoning was simple: whenever he was in Maui, it felt like the place where he needed to be. I was sad about the move because I didn't want to lose a good friend. Yes, we would still be in touch, but I thought it wouldn't be the same.

Within a few months, Harry relocated to Maui. Whenever we talked, he sounded beside himself with happiness. At first, Harry continued to work as a tour operator, but within six months of arriving in Maui, his business partners decided to buy him out. The business wasn't doing great (in fact, a year later, the tour company went out of business altogether), so Harry didn't receive the amount he needed to be financially secure. He became the general manager of a boutique hotel in Maui, and he also spent a lot of time on the beach, where he found himself captivated by the kite surfers. In his spare time, Harry started to learn how to kite surf himself, and within weeks of picking up the hobby, he bought a small kite surfing school. I had never heard him happier.

Before Harry moved there, I'd never been to Hawaii, nor did I have a great desire to go. But once Harry was there, I decided to visit him whenever I could. These trips became a routine before long, and I thought of Maui as the place I could go to recalibrate and reinvigorate myself. I basically claimed Harry's guest room as my own. Every January, I spent four days at a food show in San Francisco. From there, I would head to see Harry. Every year, I spent a little less than a week living with Harry and his family. He gave me his pickup truck when I arrived so that I could explore every beach within a one-hour radius of his house.

I'm not a car person. My cars were always a means of getting from point A to point B. So I was surprised when I climbed into the driver's seat of the pickup for the first time and felt a rush of masculinity as I turned the key and drove away. It was as if the truck had an energy that transferred to me while I was behind the wheel. I loved sitting up high, looking down at everyone while my gear was in the cargo bed (I didn't really have any gear back there, but it felt good saying that). Many of the locals drove similar trucks, although the wheels on their trucks were bigger than mine. Still, there were all the tourists who drove Jeeps and convertible Mustangs to look down on. Every once in a while, I would catch myself thinking, *Those tourists can't drive.*

If it weren't for Harry, I would have never gone to a place as far away as Maui just for myself. While I did escape a lot, all these escapes were tied to work travel, which allowed me to justify them without feeling like I was letting my family down. I could tell myself that it was practically *responsible* for me to see Harry because I was already in San Francisco and airfare to Maui was so much more affordable from the West Coast than it was from Toronto.

I usually started my time in Maui by driving to a little hippie town called Paia. Many young surfers stay there because it's a stone's throw from Hopika, Maui's surf beach. They stroll around with their long hair, flip-flops, and relaxed smiles on their faces. At one point, Paia had an issue with dog poisoning. Dogs were getting sick and acting weird for a period of months. The town was up in arms about who could be harming the dogs. Then, after a long investigation, they discovered that the dogs weren't being poisoned after all. They were just stoned from eating the butts of the joints left all over town.

I started at Paia Bay Coffee Shop, a magical, laid-back place located behind a bathing suit store in an enclosed backyard filled with large tropical plants that overhung the scattered tables. The coffee was fantastic, and so was the food—simple and tasty. I sat in a corner of the yard and soaked up people's relaxed energy.

From there, I headed over to Baldwin Beach, a beautiful stretch of sand with tranquil, turquoise-coloured water on one end and short, angry waves on the other. Local teenagers used Baldwin to bodysurf. My attempts of bodysurfing made me feel carefree and reminded me of my childhood by the Mediterranean Sea.

One time, I caught a beautiful wave that brought me very close to the sandy beach. As I rode the wave, I felt graceful and easy, just like one of the locals. As the wave fizzled, I kept swimming to shore, using the sand to move me forward. A small wave came along and helped me out. I was almost there when I made one wrong move and felt my back give. Excruciating pain penetrated my whole body. *Fuck!* My back hurt so bad, but way worse than the physical pain was the humiliation that ripped through me. I lay in the shallow water for a while and strategized how to get out of there without looking injured. I barely made it back to my towel, and when I did, I threw myself on it, trying to make it look as if I was doing so intentionally. That memory makes me laugh when I think back on it now. There I was, gliding along in that perfect moment, when the universe crashed in to remind me how human I actually was.

From Baldwin Beach, my next stop was Hopika, a surf beach where I parked the truck and climbed over a fence to walk down to a good vantage point. From there, I looked at the surfers as they figured out the waves. And then, finally, I was off to Big Beach, a beautiful, super long beach that was perfect for swimming and reading my book.

Evenings were spent sitting on Harry' balcony, drinking beer and being silly late into the night, which, in Maui, is approximately nine. It's one of those special places on earth where I found myself much more connected with natural rhythms. I tended to fall asleep when the sun went down and wake up when it rose.

When I was in Maui, I was in the closest state to just "being" as I could achieve at that point in my life—the state that all of those self-help gurus tell you to aim for.

I was lucky to have that experience as part of my yearly recalibration. That week helped keep me going for the rest of the year. I used to think, *If only I could figure out a way to have this feeling year-round.*

One year, I was on my annual visit to Maui during a time when my family's business was shaky. Our largest client had been problematic recently. Thankfully, we thought we had contained the problem and were working hard to get new customers so that we were no longer in the position of being so reliant on one large customer. With this bubbling in the background, I woke up with the sunrise one morning, did my morning stretches, and walked out to the kitchen for a double shot of espresso.

As I waited for the espresso to brew, my phone began to vibrate on the counter. It was strange to receive a call rather than a text, so I picked up the phone to see my brother's name on the screen. My heart skipped a beat; I knew I was about to hear bad news. As soon as I answered the phone and heard his voice, I could tell that he was trying to sound normal. The tone underlying that pretense of normalcy was one I'd never heard from him before.

After just a few seconds of small talk, my brother told me that our bank had informed us our ratios were out of balance due to the recent decline in sales. As a result, we needed to invest some of our personal money back into the business if we wanted to continue working with them.

My heart sank as I heard the news. This was one of my biggest fears. I had always done my best to separate my family's funds from my business investments. And now, here we were. In the end, my dad, my brother, and I all had to take large mortgages on our homes to balance the banking issue.

Having this happen while I was with Harry emphasized how stuck I was. Our lives were in such stark contrast. Here was Harry, following his dreams. He had the guts to get up and walk into his version of paradise, even though it meant stepping into the unknown. Harry had been able to do this because he believed that if he followed his heart and his instincts, everything else would sort itself out. And it did.

Then there was me. I felt trapped in my own life, as if I was scrambling to keep it all together.

I admired Harry's courage and ability to take action. To take the steps necessary to get to where he wanted to be—where he *knew*, deep down, that he should be—even when it was scary.

Watching Harry live this way made it more difficult to pretend that I was living authentically. It made it harder to ignore that I needed to take action. Something had to change, and on some level, I knew it.

On another level, though, I wasn't ready to take action just yet. And so I continued digging myself into the hole, deeper and deeper.

CHAPTER EIGHT

Shower Terror

Looking back, I can see how much pressure built up inside of me over time. It crept in bit by bit so that I didn't even realize it until I felt like I might explode. A big part of this pressure was a fear that lived in my stomach. It was always there in the background, both as the physical sensation of a mild knot in my belly and as an energetic feeling of invisible threads of stress extending out from my stomach and wrapping all around my body.

While the regular occurrences of day-to-day life might ignite a mild reaction in another person, for me they would start as a network of threads that wrap around me, lighting me up with an electric current of fear. For example, I might be walking by a playground in the park, near kids who were playing ever so happily. That sight could trigger a random memory from my own childhood, which would then result in a wave of fear suddenly overtaking my body.

I was familiar with this wave. It came to visit me once in a while with no warning. I might be sitting in a meeting or having lunch with a friend—it could wash over me anywhere, at any time, ready to attack when I least expected it.

While the stress had always been there, through my late twenties it would come and go, which made it bearable. I rode the negative feelings until they went away. But because I never did anything to resolve the core issue, the stress visited more often as time went on until it was continuous, always there in the background. It lurched in the back of my mind, and even worse, it often lapped through my entire body. By my mid-thirties, I felt as if all my muscles were bound together by a super strong rope. Today I realize the connection between the continuous stress I felt and my back issues, but I didn't then.

I was going through life's motions on the outside, while on the inside, I was stressed and miserable.

Looking back, the stress really began in my early twenties with university, and it was focussed on school. At the time, it was relatively low-key and manageable. When I graduated, that stress was channeled into my incredible drive to succeed. To me, that looked like opening a restaurant and having customers love my food. On top of that, I believed it was my responsibility to shoulder my entire family's financial well-being. More stress.

By the time I was in my mid-thirties, that drive had led me to own a business that was successful in the eyes of others. My brother, father, and I had grown a small sandwich shop in a *meh* area of town into a commercial bakery whose reach extended as far as California and western Canada. We employed two hundred people and several automated lines. But in my mind, all this was nothing. All I could see were the potential problems. Not only did real business threats occupy my mind, but so did imaginary, unrealistic ones. For the longest time, going into a supermarket to look at our products caused me incredible stress. I was afraid that I would see a new competitor on the shelves, threatening our business. I preferred to focus on developing new products; I didn't want to be on the battlefield. Thankfully, I had my brother, who handled these matters better than I did.

Every threat revolved around the fear that I could lose everything all at once. This business-related stress compounded the waves of fear that emerged from deep below the surface and sprung up when I least expected it. Not only that, but the stress got worse over time, not better. It was as if the work stress was dialed up as each year went by, even though our bakery continued doing well. In fact, my stress levels actually increased when things were going well. I was afraid, focussing on what could go wrong. During rougher times for the bakery, I actually worried less. It was as if I managed better when under threat.

All of this compounded itself into an immense load of stress that I carried with me everywhere. Tension constantly existed under the surface of my skin. My body felt as if it could never rest. Even in the moments when I was sitting with friends away from work, it was there.

Adding to this were the day-to-day tasks involved with raising three young kids in an upper-middle-class neighbourhood and the continuous comparing and competing that was done among "friends."

I felt as if I was suffocating, living my life fighting against chains that were wrapped around me. I did not acknowledge those feelings. Still, they would show up without being invited. Often, they liked to make an appearance in the early hours of the morning.

Falling asleep had always been easy for me, but sleeping through the night was a challenge. Both my grandmother and my mom had the same issue. They both kept a small radio by their bed, and when they woke up early in the morning, they would listen to the early-morning shows until they fell asleep again. I guess light sleep and early-morning wakeups run in my family.

For me, there was an extra element. In the early morning, I would suddenly wake up out of a sound sleep with my heart beating like crazy, as if it were about to jump out of my chest. My body would be covered in sweat. Worst of all was the terror I felt. Fear would take over my whole body, starting in my chest and extending all the way out to my fingers and toes.

When this happened, I sat up quickly, disoriented. As I looked around, I slowly remembered where I was and what was happening…again. I ripped the covers off to chill my sweaty body and just sat there. Ever so slowly, my heartbeat began to slow. My skin cooled and the fear slowly dissipated. It was horrible, and it usually took about an hour for me to calm down to the point where I could fall asleep again.

At first, these episodes happened infrequently. Then, as time progressed, they occurred more often. Each episode was the same.

Then, one day, these episodes moved to the daytime.

I have always enjoyed water and found it calming. As the warm water hits my head in the shower and travels down my shoulders, it feels as if it's removing both the physical and emotional dirt, sweeping it down the drain. As that residue is removed, it makes space for new thoughts and energy to enter my body. The shower has always allowed my mind to travel out of my body to faraway places, putting me in an almost hypnotic state. It has served as an escape and a place to wash both my body and my soul.

One morning, I got into the shower, looking forward to the warm water. I allowed it to hit my chest first and then slowly brought my head under the warm stream, closing my eyes and waiting for escape to wash over me as it always did. I felt so good as the water ran down my body.

And then, suddenly, I felt a wave of fear entering my body from my feet and making its way up my legs. I was way too familiar with this fear, and I knew where it was heading: straight to my chest. Instantly, fear and terror took over my entire being. My heart started beating faster, and my body tensed up and broke out in a sweat. I was sweating in the shower, and even that cleansing warm water couldn't remove it.

The shower faded into the background as the wave of fear swept me up. The world was dark and bleak. Nothing good would ever come from my life; it was all 100 percent shit. I stood there, unable to move, for who knows how long. I leaned against the wall and waited for the fear to move on.

And then, slowly, that dark wave that had come from deep within began to dissipate. I started to feel the water and my surroundings again. I quickly made my way out of the shower, dried off, and got ready to start my day. The kids, the work, the friends.

But now I knew that even my safe space wasn't safe anymore.

CHAPTER NINE

Authenticity

When I compare where I am today to where I was even eight years ago, the difference is immense. The fear and terror that constantly existed in the background have gone away completely. So has the pressure that was in my head. The waves of anxiety that snuck up on me at the most unexpected moments have dissipated. I'm not busy criticizing every word and movement that I make. When I interact with people, I see and hear them more clearly than I could before because I'm able to focus on them completely. Even my walk is different; I would go so far as to say there is a bounce in my step these days.

To me, being authentic means being comfortable in my own skin. Authenticity is when the image of what I want to say and do aligns very closely with what I actually say and do. When I find myself wanting to say something to the person standing in line next to me, I just go ahead and say it as I look directly in their eyes. And when I do this, I'm not saying something to get a response, whether it be a smile or a funny comment in return. I just say it because I felt the need to share. I mean, don't get me wrong—I do enjoy a good conversation or a laugh. But not getting those responses doesn't affect me in any way. To me, that is freedom and living authentically.

As a teenager and young adult, I was self-conscious about dancing. I needed to drink in order to free myself from the concern about what the people around me might think. Today, I can just dance without worry. (Of course, this does come at the expense of my daughter's embarrassment, but I'm also sending her a message in these moments: *just be yourself*.)

Had I not discovered this new way of being, I truly think my body would have suffered from various ailments. At a certain point, I would have run out of energy to continue hiding out from everyone I loved and from myself. Today, I am as close to freedom as I can imagine being. Don't get me wrong. I still have some issues to deal with. But I'm much closer than I used to be.

Once upon a time, my day-to-day life felt like I was trying to function in the world while sick with a never-ending fever. I was there, but not 100 percent. My body was too busy fighting the virus to function correctly.

I'm sure I would have kept on living like this for much longer if my brother hadn't asked me to go to the airport to pick up a childhood friend of ours, Michael, who was visiting from Boston.

I picked Michael up and drove him back to my parents' home so that he could say hello to my mother. As we drove, Michael told me about all the changes he had made in his life. Until recently, he had been a midlevel manager for a hotel chain. Michael had been working his way up the corporate ladder and suffering in the process. A couple of months before our visit, Michael quit his job and began taking courses to figure out his next step.

I couldn't help but notice that Michael seemed happy and different. I was captivated, and before I knew it, two hours had passed. Our conversation had lasted all the way from the airport to my parents' kitchen table, where we continued to talk.

Towards the end of our conversation, Michael told me about a three-day course he'd taken that had helped him realize how stuck and miserable he was in life. I wasn't surprised to hear this because Michael had complained about his job for years—the issues he had with his superiors and all the irrational customers he had to deal with on a regular basis. It was clear that Michael's job had caused him grief. Michael's goals weren't aligned with what he actually wanted. Once Michael realized this, he pressed the reset button. The two of us discussed how little we had invested in ourselves up to this point. Instead, we invested in *things*—homes, cars, clothes. But not ourselves.

To me, Michael seemed quite different than before. His energy was entirely altered. Our conversation stuck with me, but most of all, I was deeply impacted by how full of hope and plans for the future Michael seemed to be. I wanted to feel like that too.

As I sat in my office the next day, my heart started beating faster. I knew that feeling all too well by this point, and it suddenly dawned on me that if I continued on this route, my body would ultimately pay the price for it—and it would probably be a big one. In that moment, I realized I had to do something.

In some ways, these were conscious thoughts, and in other ways, they were subconscious. I had so many layers within myself that were holding onto different realities and secrets. The outermost layer was my external, visible, work-related stress. But there was something else deeper down—something that I knew in my core but I was unable to consciously acknowledge. Still, on some level, I knew that this murky, unacknowledged stress was at the core of all my problems.

I spent years ignoring the real cause of my stress and discontent for the simple reason that acknowledging it was too scary and painful. If I acknowledged it, I would have to act on it. Things in my life would have to shift in significant ways. I would have to swim out into uncharted waters. So instead of acknowledging that stress and the understanding that it pointed to, my mind latched onto other stresses as a way of creating noise and distracting me from the real issue at hand.

As I sat in the executive chair in my office with my heart racing, the core source of stress moved upward, one level closer to the surface. One step closer to my everyday consciousness. It was close, but not quite there—I experienced it as a sense of fear and shame rather than a specific understanding of what was happening. Still, I knew that *something* was emerging. And whatever it was, I was scared of it.

A few days after seeing Michael and that moment of panic in my office, I decided to register for a weekend seminar designed to help attendees reprogram themselves and change their core realities and perceptions. It felt like the only action I could take to make some headway on whatever I was feeling.

As I filled out the registration form, I came to a question that asked what I was looking to gain from the weekend. I thought long and hard about that question. It seemed like a big one to me—bigger than just a question on a registration form for a seminar. It seemed like it had something to do with this thing that was bubbling up inside of me. The phrase "peace and quiet" came to mind, but that wasn't quite right. I thought maybe I wanted more wealth so that I could feel more financially stable. The business was growing, but we kept reinvesting funds, which meant that the idea of financial security was always on my mind. Still, I knew enough to understand that money would only resolve the stress in one area of my life.

By the time I finished filling out that form several days later, I was still dancing around the core misalignment in my life, but at least I was getting closer to it. That felt promising in some ways, but in another way, it felt scary. I made a conscious decision to have faith that everything would be okay in the long run. I wanted to believe that things would work out for me, just like they seemed to be working out for Michael.

The seminar was interesting, and I was especially taken with the gentleman leading it. He was incredibly skilled, and I was amazed by how he so clearly touched people. With just a few questions, he helped my fellow attendees realize new truths about their lives. One of the main things we discussed was the importance of being authentic with ourselves and the people around us. From deep within me, I heard a voice telling me that I was not being authentic with myself.

As I heard that voice from within, an invisible switch inside me clicked to the *on* position.

The weekend helped me a lot when it came to work stress, which was a big deal. Immediately, my stress level went from a nine out of ten down to a six. It felt like a fucking miracle! As time progressed, my stress levels dropped even lower. That's not to say that the stress disappeared entirely. Work stress still appeared once in a while, depending on the business environment I was in. For example, new competition always set off alarms inside me. Or if I heard a rumour about a food trend that didn't align with our products, I would immediately jump to imagining a great financial loss. The good thing about me is that this type of stress pushes me into overdrive. I respond by creating new and innovative products and advertising and doing what it takes to grow the business. That meant that our business grew, especially in the face of imaginary threats.

I don't exactly know why my business-related stress decreased as a result of that seminar. I think that some kind of reprograming occurred. I realized I'd chosen to be in the situations I found myself in. With this, I learned that I had the freedom to choose both where I was and how I responded to things. For example, usually as I sat in meetings, I spent the whole time thinking, *I hate this meeting, and I don't want to be here.* At the first meeting

I attended after that weekend, that same familiar thought crept into my mind, but this time I caught it and replaced it with, *I want to be in this meeting. I choose to be here.* That simple switch alone had an impact on my outlook.

Learning to manage my stress felt incredible—almost magical, even. And that was amazing. However, even though my levels of stress diminished, that weekend course had also served to turn my authenticity switch on. And that was problematic.

I now very consciously realized that there was an issue I had been avoiding my entire life. The realization came ever so delicately. I wasn't ready to name it yet, but I *was* ready to acknowledge that more work was required. I knew that I could not continue with life as I had so far.

The truth that I'd been holding onto so tightly in my core began making its way to the surface, closer and closer. It was as if alleviating all that work stress had made enough room to allow deeper issues to start moving up. I knew it was coming to the surface, and that scared me.

CHAPTER TEN

Free Choice

A couple of years after the course, I was still intent on trying to be more conscious of everything I did, both big and small. Interestingly, I found that the more aware I became of the smaller behaviours, the more all my behaviour changed. It was like the smaller stuff acted as a training ground for me to examine my thoughts and interact with the world in a new way.

For example, every New Year, like clockwork, I received a present from the nice Korean couple who had bought our retail store. Each year, the present was the same: a box of tasty Korean pears and a box of gourmet tea. I always gave the pears to my team. The tea was left to linger on my desk for weeks with all of the other junk I constantly collected. At some point a few months later,

I discarded the tea unopened, along with all the other clutter on my desk.

This particular year, a couple of months after receiving the tea, I walked into my office and was annoyed to be greeted by the usual mess on my desk. I reached for the first thing I saw, which was the tea. Without thinking, I tossed it in the garbage. As the box left my hand, it suddenly struck me how automatic that action was. Immediately, I regretted what I had done. *This is such an entitled, shitty move!* I thought. I reached into the garbage bin to extract the tea and then placed it on my desk and looked at it. I thought about how this nice couple had taken the time to buy this tea, write a nice card, and send it to my office. And here I was, not even taking the time to taste their thoughtful gift. I decided to fight my automatic reaction and give the tea a chance.

Off I went to the kitchen, where I tore off the plastic wrapping and opened the box of tea. I assumed it was supposed to be good for me because the sachets were filled with a grey powder that didn't look particularly appetizing. In most situations, I make up my mind about whether I like an object or experience the first moment I see it. From that point forward, all my actions are aligned with that initial (often mistaken) decision. Not only that, but I also make sure the world knows how I feel about that thing or experience.

Nonetheless, even though I wasn't overwhelmed with positive feelings about this grey tea, I made the conscious decision to take the sachet out of the box and place it in a mug. As I waited for the water to boil, I made myself focus on the effort this lovely couple had put into getting this tea to me.

When the water was boiling, I lifted the kettle and poured the hot water into my mug. I watched as the water quickly turned the same greyish hue as the contents in the sachet. Again, I caught myself thinking that the tea must taste gross, but I made a conscious decision to stop the negative thoughts. I told myself that I should try the tea before deciding whether I liked it.

I walked back to my office with the tea. After it had cooled a bit, I lifted the mug and tasted it. It wasn't good... but it wasn't bad, either. I slowly drank the tea as I continued working. It was a small thing, but I felt happy that I had caught myself in action and seized the opportunity to break my habitual behaviour.

As I was driving home later that day, I couldn't stop thinking about that tea and the fact that so many of my actions and judgments were robotic. I had caught myself in this one moment, but how many other moments had I done this precise thing without thinking twice? How many experiences and people had I missed out on because of my tendency to jump to snap judgments? How many other behaviours were so embedded in me that I didn't even notice I was performing them?

On that drive, I decided to start looking for other inroads where I could go against my nature. I wanted to discover where I might be holding myself back and limiting my experience of life without even realizing it.

Food seemed like a safe place to experiment more with this, and immediately the drink that I hated the most came to mind: coffee. Since I was a child, I had been surrounded by coffee drinkers. My dad, in particular, was fueled by it; he loved deep, dark Turkish coffee the most.

I thought back to one time as a young teenager when I had gone with my dad to visit an Arabic family in northern

Israel. Coffee is a staple in the Arabic tradition, and guests are always offered dark, black, very sweet coffee. So, of course, on that visit, my dad and I were both offered coffee. I panicked, knowing that it is a great insult in the Arabic tradition for a guest to refuse food or drink. I watched in horror as a tray loaded with small coffee glasses was passed around. The woman serving it looked at me with a smile, as if she knew the turmoil that was happening inside my head. I extended my arm and took the glass. It was hot. I looked around the room as everyone brought their cup up to their lips and began drinking. Everyone seemed happy, except for me. I brought the glass to my lips and sipped just a little. It was disgusting, simultaneously overly sweet and bitter.

Still, I couldn't refuse the drink because I didn't want to insult our hosts. So, I kept on holding the cup long after everyone else had finished their coffee. As I was listening to the adults speak, the woman who had served us came over and took the still-full cup out of my hand. I could see an understanding smile in her eyes.

A few years later, I was in the army, tasked with the very important job of guarding a pile of sand. It was three in the morning, and I still had a couple more hours to go. I was exhausted.

We got a five-minute break, during which we could get something to drink and use the washroom. For most people, coffee was the ideal beverage in times like this. It was warm and caffeinated. I fought back my disdain and decided to force myself to drink the coffee. I told myself that even if I didn't like it, I could choke it down for the sake of being warm and awake.

I entered a battered structure, headed to the coffee pot, and poured myself a cup, adding a couple of spoonsful of sugar to help with the taste. The cup warmed my cold hands. I lifted the cup to my nose and breathed in deeply. Oddly, I always liked the smell of coffee. I paused for a moment before I sipped, feeling anxious as I anticipated the bad taste. I took a swig and, within a split second, recoiled in disgust, made a face, and spat out the coffee with a grunt of displeasure. It was all very dramatic. The guys around me looked up with surprise. I poured the coffee out, washed the cup to rid it of the coffee flavor, and poured myself some warm water instead.

Clearly, coffee and I were not meant to share a future together. Yet, at that moment in my car, I knew I needed to challenge my disdain for coffee.

The next day, I was determined to go ahead with this little experiment of mine. I dropped my bag off in my office and headed to the kitchen. I decided to go with the darkest and most concentrated coffee I could: espresso. If I was going to succeed, I had to go big! I placed the little espresso cup under the spout. Thankfully, it was one of those automated machines that doesn't require much skill to operate. I pressed the blinking button, and the machine woke up and began humming and clicking. Within seconds, the warm, thick coffee began flowing out of the spout.

Once the cup was full, I added one teaspoon of sugar to break the bitterness. Then I stood there in the office kitchen, staring down at the espresso. I thought about how much I had hated coffee every time I had tried it before, and then I reminded myself that I was consciously deciding to change my attitude. I decided to like the espresso. To reinforce that, I said, "I am going to love this coffee!" out loud three times. With that, I lifted the small mug to my mouth and slowly but surely drank all the espresso.

As I put the mug back on the counter, I realized that I hadn't gagged, and my face hadn't scrunched up. Somehow, coffee wasn't disgusting to me anymore. Sure, it wasn't great—but I didn't hate it. A rush of energy raced through my body, and that feeling kept me going for the next few hours.

But more than that, this experience taught me something about the power of words and intention. If I decided I was going to try (and like) something, the chances of me liking it were much higher than if I went into the experience with a negative attitude.

The next day I decided to conquer coffee once again. I repeated the same ritual I had the previous day, including telling myself out loud that I was going to love the coffee. As I drank that second espresso, what do you know? I fell in love.

Becoming more aware of my behaviour in smaller moments like this made me notice my larger behavioural patterns and habits I had fallen into and repeated time and time again without even noticing. As human beings, we all do this because it makes it easier for us to put the majority of our decision-making energy into the more crucial decisions in our lives. For me, that energy tends to go into important things, like choosing what colour shirt I should wear for the day. I kid you not, this choice sometimes takes me up to ten minutes on an already busy morning. Is that a wise distribution of my decision energy? I mean, I would argue yes. But the main point here is that I can allocate this energy towards my clothing decisions because I automate so many other behaviours in my life.

Once I started to look for these patterns, I realized I could usually identify them by recognizing moments where time had gone by without me even realizing it was passing. Driving is a great example of automatic behaviour. I can't even begin to count how many times I got into the car at home and, seemingly within a split second, found myself at the bakery, when in reality, forty minutes had disappeared. Once I realized that, I started to be more mindful of my driving time and how my automatic behaviour was conditioned to click in from the moment I turned on the radio and the morning show host's voice filled the car. It was at that moment that I tended to disappear into another world.

Once I started to understand that these behaviours existed, I also began to see that I'd been living my life inside a glass box. I was under the illusion that I operated with free choice, yet I was confined by invisible walls that I had erected. These walls allowed me to see outside and interact with others, and they provided the illusion that I was free, yet I wasn't able to move beyond the safe confines of my glass prison. I just thought I wasn't a prisoner because I could see the larger world through my glass.

I started to shake up my routine more and more. At first, it took a lot of concentration. For example, on my drive, I would often catch myself as my hand reached out to turn on the car radio when I'd intended to make the commute in silence. Through the simple act of leaving the radio off, I was able to discover my own thoughts. It felt as if they were awake again after being in a deep sleep from all the information I had been distracting myself with. Other times, I opted to listen to music from my own library rather than the gloomy news or radio stations. The music I chose put me in different moods rather than allowing a random selection of information or music on the radio to set the tone for my day. Driving to work became a game. Along with changing the environment in my car, I also chose different routes instead of obediently following whatever orders the all-knowing Waze doled out to me.

I discovered other limiting patterns in my life, and over time, I also realized that automatic behaviour can be beneficial and healthy in certain circumstances. Take swimming, for example. For most of my life, I would not have considered myself an athletic person. Early on, my asthma and allergies convinced me that staying home was always a better option for me than exercising in the great outdoors. Then a friend introduced me to swimming. I began swimming for ten minutes at a time and felt like I was going to die by the end of it. Nonetheless, I appreciated that swimming didn't cause me to sweat, and because it's a solo sport, my lack of coordination wasn't reflected back at me through the horrified looks on the faces of my teammates. I also liked how my muscles responded to swimming. It turned out that maybe I wasn't doomed to be the skinny, lanky Middle Eastern guy after all. Maybe I could instead be a somewhat toned, lanky Middle Eastern guy.

What started as painful ten-minute swimming sessions twice a week slowly but surely became more extended and frequent. Today, I swim for just under an hour a few times a week. Over time, it has become both a mental and physical escape for me. I've gotten to the point where even when I have second thoughts about going to the pool, I make a conscious decision to allow the automatic muscle memory of getting into the car, driving to the gym, parking, trudging through the snow, and walking to the changing room to take over. It feels almost as if I somehow find myself in the pool on those days. It's the same thing that used to happen to me when I commuted on autopilot, only now the effect is positive because I've acknowledged and *chosen* this automatic behaviour.

I allow this to happen because I now understand that even if I feel lousy or stressed when I lower myself into the water, that feeling or thought will dissipate within the first ten minutes of my swim. If, on the other hand, I decide to fight that automatic behaviour and skip swimming, I will instead feel stressed out for the rest of the day. Over the years, I have made the conscious choice to treat swimming as I now treat drinking coffee: it's an addiction that I accept. I am aware that I depend on it, and that's okay. It serves me.

Most important in all this, I've learned, is the notion of continuing to challenge my accepted reality. I believe this is what being human is all about. People always talk about how humans are different from other animals because we have free will. Yet so many of us settle for a life of routine and automatic behaviour. That's all good and fine if it's what you want and *choose* for your life experience. But I came to learn that if I wanted to really feel, smell, and *experience* life, I had to make the decision to continuously challenge my automatic behaviours. My personal rule is that once I challenge an automatic behaviour, I can make the choice to either replace it or keep it. The point is in the challenge. It's in seeing and breaking through the glass wall.

Humans tend to fall back into our routines. They become a crutch and a glass prison of our own making. They are familiar and give us a sense of safety and, sometimes, control. We need those things. However, to maximize our potential in this life, I believe that every once in a while, we also need to challenge those patterns. Who knows? You might try this only to find out you're in alignment with your unconscious behaviours. In that case, the challenging becomes an affirmation. In other cases, you can discard the old, stale, limiting behaviours to allow space for new energy.

CHAPTER ELEVEN

Couples Therapy

I found that the more aware I became of my own patterns and ingrained behaviours, the angrier I became with the people I was closest to. Most of all, my anger towards Michelle grew because she was the closest person to me. It was easy to blame her for the gap I was beginning to see in my alignment with who I really was. No matter what, she couldn't do anything right. I didn't always share my frustrations with her, but she definitely noticed that I wasn't myself. More than once, she asked me if I was okay. Each time she asked, I brushed her off, telling her I was stressed, work was busy, or I hadn't slept properly the night before.

It was all bullshit, with the intention of making the questions go away. But even when the questions went away, the anger didn't. On the contrary, it got worse. I was so annoyed with Michelle.

As this was happening, I didn't think about the future or where the path I was on was leading. I didn't have the ability to see the big picture—I was too busy making it through each difficult and frustrating day, one day at a time. But I *did* know that I couldn't continue to pretend I was happy. The basement gave me space to think and contemplate. The lack of visual stimuli allowed me to go inward and tackle the issues that had begun to surface.

The kids never said anything about my move to the basement, probably because it happened gradually. I'm sure they *did* notice that their parents' relationship had begun to suffer. Both Michelle and I were very aware of not letting our differences affect the kids. They came first, even though both of us were hurting. As for the rest of the world, only our very close circle of friends knew there were any issues. The rest of the world continued to see us as the perfect family.

Eventually, Michelle and I decided that the status quo could not go on for any longer, so we decided to go to couples therapy. Maybe that would help. I needed and wanted help.

Our first therapist was very warm and friendly—and, I thought, annoying. I didn't want to feel her warmth or friendliness. I didn't want or need understanding. I required an impartial person to act as a mirror for my bullshit. I needed someone to shine a light on our issues without judgment. I needed help bringing to the surface what was happening, and I needed the time and tools to deal with it. A friendly therapist doesn't work for me, although I understand why it would for others.

Each time we talked to the therapist, we reached a dead end in the conversation. Outside of that, I don't remember much about those meetings. I'm pretty sure I told Michelle and the therapist that I had changed and my wife hadn't; therefore, we were not "in the same place" as people. In many ways, that was true. It was mean of me to say that in therapy because I was secretly setting Michelle up, as if the challenges in our relationship were somehow her fault. I didn't plan to do this; it just happened. The therapist saw a successful man and a stay-at-home mom, and I assume she thought my assessment of our situation was accurate.

Obviously, those sessions didn't last. It turned out that the only person I fooled by placing the blame on Michelle was myself.

This pattern repeated itself with a series of three more couples therapists over a period of six months, at which point we decided to take a break from the sessions. Not surprisingly, our relationship wasn't stable. There were a couple of highs here and there and many lows. Nothing was resolved.

I remained in the basement, and Michelle and I continued to coparent our kids the best we could. We were civil to each other. The façade of normalcy was still in place, tattered though it was.

One evening, Michelle and I were out celebrating something or other—I couldn't tell you what—at one of the hottest restaurants in the city. I had been looking forward to checking the place out, but once we got there, every aspect of the food and service was lost on me. I was miserable inside, and needless to say, dinner was tense.

As we drove home, Michelle tried to ask me questions. I lost it at her, even though none of my discontent was really aimed at her. It was aimed at the world. I could hear the frustration and rage in my own voice. Tears burned in my eyes as I yelled out the car window in frustration. Once I was done, that all-too-familiar silence descended over the car once again.

I felt so alone. I considered the option of living apart from my wife. For a split second, I felt good about that possibility. But then, in the next breath, I thought about *not* living under the same roof as my kids. Just the thought of it made me cringe. I couldn't imagine that reality.

It felt like there was no hope.

Down in the basement, where it was quiet and I was alone, that thing I had been trying to avoid began making its way up to the surface. Now it was lurking there, just under the surface. I could tell it was there, and now I even knew what it was. I still couldn't say the words. But I could think them.

In the safety of my basement, I was watching gay pornography.

It hadn't started like this. It began by occasionally looking at the men in straight porn. I rationalized to myself that it was straight sex, so it was all good. As time passed, my porn habits shifted. I started to watch one gay scene after watching straight porn. Then it got to the point where I would watch all gay porn, with one straight scene thrown in for good measure.

Over time, I didn't even bother with the straight porn anymore.

Okay, I told myself. *I am bisexual. I still have a wife, and I enjoy having sex with her.* My wife became my heterosexual shield for the world and for myself. As long as I didn't say the g-word, none of this was real. It was just thoughts. I could think about things, and it didn't mean anything. Everyone does that, right? I think about many things. I've been thinking about things my whole life.

Writing this today, it sounds ridiculous. I can now see that I was lying to myself, as if I had a lawyer in my head, building the case for why I wasn't gay. And then, one day, the lawyer quit his job. There was all this curiosity in my mind, but I'd never had the guts or ability to act on it in the real world. I told myself that as long as it existed only in my head, it wasn't real.

A day or two after my outburst in the car, I was sitting alone on my single bed in the basement. It seemed that I had run out of options. My fingers made their way to the computer on the desk and began typing. The words "gay father Toronto" appeared on the screen. I pressed enter. *It's okay*, I told myself. *The computer screen is just an extension of my mind.* These are just words. Mind you, those words seemed more real as they appeared on the screen, as if the computer could now read my mind.

Several options appeared on the screen. I scrolled down and then back up again. My eyes zeroed in on the Gay Fathers of Toronto, a group that met twice a month at the community centre downtown, which was located right next to the gay village. Apparently I wasn't the only person in this position. I quickly looked to see when the next meeting was and then slammed the computer shut again.

There. It wasn't real anymore. I was normal again.

For the moment, at least.

CHAPTER TWELVE

Gay Fathers of Toronto

It took me about a month to actually go to a meeting. I finally summoned up the courage on a warm, late-summer evening.

I was so nervous as I got into my car to head downtown. I made sure I had a baseball cap on to disguise myself—but not my company hat, lest it give my identity away. In addition to the cap, I was also buried under an oversized grey hoodie. A knot sat firmly in my stomach for the entire thirty-minute drive. As I drove, I looked out the window, observing the view in an attempt to prevent myself from thinking about anything.

Those thirty minutes went by so fast. Too fast.

I reached the community centre and then drove past it as if I were heading somewhere else. A couple of blocks later, I turned onto a side street and found parking. I wanted to make sure the car was far enough away from the community centre that no one would link me to it if anyone saw my car. After I parked, I remained in the driver's seat with both hands on the steering wheel at ten and two, just like my driving teacher had taught me. I stayed there for a little while and then took a big breath and stepped out of the car and into whatever was coming next.

Despite my baseball cap and hoodie, I kept my head down. I even changed my walk a little.

I was about twenty minutes early, so I walked past the centre and sat on the ledge of the pavement around the corner. I chewed my gum with extra vigor, trying not to think about anything. I felt the same way I had before that first presentation in the army: a buildup of pressure inside of me, nausea, and a rapid heartbeat. Oddly, buried under all that stress, there was also a tiny bit of excitement.

I waited in that spot on the pavement until one minute before seven. I didn't want to be early; I didn't want to sit there in silence with the other gay fathers of Toronto—or, even worse, to sit there and talk with the others. I wanted to be invisible at the meeting.

As I stood up to go inside, I realized I'd gotten hot and sweaty from sitting outside all bundled up on a nice summer day. I could feel the sweat on my forehead, which made me even more nervous. It was not a good look. I looked down to avoid making eye contact with anyone, opened the door, and walked towards the information booth. Out of the corner of my eye, I could see a few people hanging around, chatting on the main floor. A few more steps, and I was standing in front of the man working the booth. I lifted my head just a little bit, careful not to make eye contact.

"How can I help you?" a friendly voice asked.

I leaned forward. "What room is Gay Fathers in?" I asked as quietly as possible.

He pointed me in the direction of the elevator and explained how to get to the room from there.

"Thanks," I whispered.

There was no way I was taking the elevator with another person, so I headed to the stairs instead. I didn't want to be late and risk everyone stopping mid-meeting to lift their eyes towards me as I entered the room, so now I had to run. Running up the stairs made me sweat even more. By the time I reached the third floor, I was a complete mess, with sweat visible all over my face. In fact, my entire body was soaking. I could only hope it wouldn't seep through my clothes in the course of the meeting.

Thankfully, the room was close to the stairway. I felt like I was on another planet, and my goal was to have minimal contact with the locals. It's not as if I didn't know gay people. I even had a couple of gay friends. I did. Looking back, I wonder why I was so apprehensive of the other people in the room that day—people who could actually *relate* to my situation. It doesn't seem like a big deal as I sit here writing in a very gay-friendly café. But of course, I had to take many steps to get here.

The door to the room was half open. I walked in slowly to find eight people who were chatting and seemed to know each other. The guy who seemed to be the organizer greeted me with a big hello. I nodded my head in return. From that point forward, he left me alone. I guess he had experience with guys in my situation—the quiet guys who wore hoodies and caps on warm summer days. A few more men walked in after me, and the meeting began.

It started with a welcome, and then everyone was asked to introduce themselves to the group. I was chewing my gum so vigorously that it began to fall apart in my mouth. Never before in my gum-chewing life had that happened. I guess the gum was no match for the extra heat in my body and the intense, rapid chewing. When it was my turn to introduce myself, I told the others in the room that my name was Danny. For some reason, as I said my name, I placed my hand on my mouth, and the decomposed gum got stuck and stretched all the way from my mouth to my hand as I tried to disconnect it. Someone handed me a paper towel to help get it off.

From that point on, things got even worse. I sat quietly in my corner, listening to the conversation going on around me. The stories that a few of the participants told were horrible. One guy cried as he talked about how he had been excommunicated from both his home and church after coming out to his family in rural Ontario. Another guy's wife told him that he was a pervert and that she was worried for their kids' safety. She asked him to leave their home. And so on. I thought the guys who sought help from groups like this were probably in worst-case scenarios and therefore needed the support. At least I desperately hoped that was the case.

Even though I was in a room with men who were in a similar situation to my own, I still didn't feel as if I belonged. They seemed weak and broken. I didn't feel weak or broken, even though I was. Maybe I viewed them in this light because they were emotional about their situations. I was able to keep things inside and not show the world the contradictions that existed in my soul. Perhaps that was the result of the lack of affection or emotions on my father's side of the family and the stiff upper lip on my mother's British side.

It wasn't just this room, though. When I thought about it, I realized that I had never met a gay person I could relate to. Most, if not all, gay people were somehow different than me. At least, that was how I felt then. Today, I know there are many gay men like me. They just don't stand out in a crowd because they don't lead with their sexuality. To them, being gay is just one of their many character traits.

As I sat there, my world darkened. I felt more alone than ever. I didn't think Michelle would be vindictive, but who knows how a person will behave when they are deeply angry or hurt? I couldn't be sure of anything.

The meeting came to an end, and the moderator invited us all to join him for a beer at a nearby bar. I stood up quickly and got out of there. By this point, I was so defeated that the stress and sweat were gone. There was nothing left except for a little despair.

I can't recall the rest of that day.

By the next day, I felt a little better and had gained a little more perspective. I went back to the Gay Fathers of Toronto website and read some personal stories that actually had happy endings.

What now? I asked myself. As I gazed at the screen, I saw a tab of recommended therapists who specialized in sexuality.

CHAPTER THIRTEEN

The Experience

It took me a few days to connect with Derek, one of the therapists from the Gay Fathers of Toronto site.

In the days after the meeting, I was in a haze, mostly operating on autopilot in all areas of my life. I created a protective shield between my feelings and my day-to-day life. I didn't allow myself to think about anything. I just focussed on the things I had to do—and next up was meeting with a therapist.

I knew that each of these steps would lead me to the next, just like the Gay Fathers meeting had led me to the therapist, but I couldn't deal with the thought of more than one step at the time.

Finally, I sent Derek an email introducing myself and asking to schedule a meeting. His response came fairly quickly, and we scheduled our first meeting for the following week.

I was still scared and stressed out after I scheduled the meeting, but I also felt a stir of excitement. Could this work? Was it possible? These thoughts existed in a completely separate part of my brain than the section where the fear and anxiety lived. It was as if a new area of my brain had formed for the purpose of creating a space for a new reality, separate from my negative thoughts. Each side of my brain pretended that the other didn't exist.

Before I went to my first solo session with Derek, I told Michelle that I had decided to go to therapy on my own. "I need to work on myself," I told her. A hopeful look crossed Michelle's face. She nodded and said that she supported me and hoped it would help us. Her reaction made me feel shitty. I didn't want to give Michelle the illusion of hope, despite the fact that I didn't have any clear answers for myself either. I just knew that I had to keep exploring and digging.

My therapy appointment was scheduled for the middle of the day, just before lunchtime. I wanted to have some time after the session so I could go somewhere and be alone with my thoughts.

Derek's office was located on the second floor of a small house that was divided into several offices. I walked into the house just on time after waiting in the car outside in hopes that I would avoid running into his previous client. I didn't want to be identified as someone who was going to see a therapist who specialized in sexuality issues. I was so self-conscious that I felt if anyone saw me there, it would be the equivalent of carrying a big sign over my head that read, "This guy is dealing with his sexuality!" How embarrassing.

When I knocked on Derek's door, I was greeted by a forty-something guy who seemed pleasant but didn't otherwise strike me in any specific way. He just seemed to be a regular guy. I think I was expecting someone who looked like a Hollywood actor playing the part of a therapist—perhaps wearing a tweed jacket and designer glasses, maybe with a pipe on the table for good measure. But no. It turned out that Derek was just a normal-looking guy. That was fortunate because it allowed me to focus on myself rather than analyzing him to death, seeking out his weaknesses and faults as I usually did.

Derek's office was like him—normal. It was a little shabby yet comfortable and warm. There was a couch, and I figured that was where I was supposed to sit based on the tissue box on the coffee table in front of it.

Derek briefly introduced himself and asked me some basic background questions. I don't know what I was expecting, but nothing noteworthy happened in the course of our conversation, and the hour went by quickly.

As Derek and I continued to meet, it occurred to me that he seemed to have no agenda. He just listened. At times he would ask a question, but never anything too probing. This approach worked for me. Derek let me speak about different aspects of my life. I shared various stories and frustrations, and often our conversation went in circles. Still, they weren't unproductive. By listening to me and letting me take my time, Derek gained my trust, and the defences that I usually employed—cynicism, humour, or finding reasons that the person sitting across from me was not qualified to do their job—took a back seat.

I wasn't used to interactions like this—especially with therapists. I thought I could fool anyone with words. After all, that was what I had done for as long as I could remember, dating back to the days when I could persuade my mom to buy my bullshit so that I could stay home from school. I always made sure that I played off the other person's weaknesses—I understood from a young age that my health was my mother's. Likewise, when I was in the army, I learned the language and managed to get out of kitchen duty by making them think I was allergic to the water by dipping my hands into some soap that made me break out in a rash. The same sort of scenarios had occurred time and time again with Michelle. I needed those tricks so that I could function in everyday life. At least, that was what I told myself.

But I didn't use any of my usual tricks with Derek.

During our fifth session, I told him about my unhappy relationship with my wife and the meeting I had attended at the Gay Fathers of Toronto.

"Alon, are you gay?" Derek asked me point-blank.

No one had ever asked me that question directly before—although, thinking back, I recall a couple of times when people thought I was gay. One time when I was visiting my brother in Berlin, I went out for a beer with an artist friend of his. We were sitting at a busy, noisy bar, deeply immersed in a philosophical conversation. At a certain point, my friend got up to use the washroom. I stayed at the bar, feeling very good about the moment I found myself in. I noticed a girl at a table across from me looking in my direction, so I smiled at her. She got up and approached me with a smile on her face.

She leaned in close to me and said, with a heavy German accent, "I have noticed you from my seat, and I just wanted to tell you that you are beautiful and that it's perfect that you are gay." With that, she returned to her table.

I wasn't shocked or that surprised by this unsolicited commentary. In fact, I felt as if I had just received a compliment. It felt good to be noticed—especially by a complete stranger. Of course, the main part of the compliment I absorbed was "you are beautiful." I ignored the gay part, even though I'd heard it perfectly well. Thinking back on it today, though, maybe her words gave me a tiny boost towards acknowledging who and what I am.

A few seconds later, my friend returned, and we were back at it.

The second time I was "mistaken" for gay was when Michelle and I went to an after-hours gay bar with a few friends from out of town. As I was checking our coats, a cute young guy who was most likely high as a kite grabbed my arm and swept me away in an attempt to get me to dance. It was fair enough for him to assume that a guy standing at coat check at a gay dance bar was gay. I just went for it for a few seconds. Looking back, it's odd that this didn't rattle me. I guess it was because my identity was buried so deep and I was so intent on avoiding it.

And now, here I was. I paused for a moment before replying to Derek's question. "I don't know," I finally answered. "I've never been with a man. I've been married since I was twenty-four years old, and I was with my wife for a few years before that. I have never been with anyone other than her in that time."

Then it was Derek's turn to pause. I could see that he was processing what I had just said. He didn't challenge me or probe any further. All he said was, "Well, maybe you should try to be with a man. Maybe you owe it to your wife to find out."

I left Derek's office that day with a sense of both pressure and excitement. What he said made sense to me. I would do this for Michelle! Of course, now I know that I was actually doing it for myself.

It didn't even occur to me to tell Michelle what was happening or what I was thinking. She knew that I was going to a therapist, but she wasn't aware that I was talking to a therapist about my sexuality. There was no need for her to know that I was gay before I found out for myself if I actually was.

Over the past eighteen years, I had never cheated on my wife for many reasons, most of all because it's very difficult for me to lie. I knew that if I were to cheat, I would suffer through many sleepless, guilt-ridden nights. The second biggest reason was the health aspect of straying. I'm somewhat of a hypochondriac and would never expose Michelle to any kind of disease. But since we weren't sleeping together at this point, it was the perfect time for me to experiment. I also knew that our relationship was at its end. Finding out who I was needed to take precedence over all other commitments. At least, that was how I rationalized it to myself.

Although I had never strayed, it wasn't as if I'd never thought about it. Over the years, there were a couple of times when just one touch was all it would have taken for a full-on affair to ignite. The tension was built up to the degree that it was almost a physical thing. I wasn't in love with either of these people, but I did enjoy their attention, and they provided my mind with an escape from what felt like the torture of my day-to-day life.

Of course, both of these instances were with women. I wonder what would have happened if they had been with men. Would I have been able to turn away? In retrospect, I don't think I would have. Most likely, I would have collapsed and given myself away. But that hadn't been the case, so I never took action on any opportunities out of respect for the commitment I'd made to my wife.

Now I knew what I wanted to do, but I didn't know how to go about meeting someone. Not only had I been out of the dating game for a long time, but I'd never been with a man before. As is always the case when you need to know something, I searched online. Fairly quickly, I discovered all I needed to know about dating apps for men looking for hookups.

I downloaded my app of choice and began answering all the questions. They started out easy enough, with things like height and weight. But then, very quickly, I got confused. *What tribes do you belong to? What do you like?* (I had a feeling that question wasn't referring to my favourite culinary dishes.) So I just wrote the truth, plain and simple: *I am new to this. Need help figuring things out.*

Next came photos. I was definitely not fit enough to compete with most of the guys on the app, and I wasn't willing to post a photo of my face for all to see. Aside from the fact that I was still married, I was also still telling myself that I wasn't even sure I was gay; I was just checking things out. After a lot of searching, I found a photo from a fairly recent beach vacation. I carefully cropped off my head and posted the photo with my profile.

And then I waited. I had no clue what to expect, but it was exciting to look at photos of all the guys on the app. I was a little worried that everyone seemed to be younger than me. How could I compete? They all looked so much better than me.

I put the phone down, wondering how long it would take to find a willing participant. Would anyone even respond? And if so, would I be attracted to them?

Shockingly, it didn't take too long before my phone vibrated and a response came in. Within an hour, I was chatting with a couple of guys. It was really nice. The conversation was easy, and even though we had met on an app designed for quick encounters, I managed to connect with guys who were also interested in talking. I quickly found that it was easy for me to communicate with guys. We spoke the same language, and there was flow, directness, and surprisingly, sensitivity. I never thought conversations with strangers could feel so natural.

One of the guys I talked to seemed to be particularly nice, confident, and understanding. I was struck by how easygoing he seemed. Strangely, I can't remember this guy's name anymore, so for the purposes of this story, we'll call him Josh. Josh suggested that I come over to his place the next day, just to chill. As he put it, "No pressure, dude."

When the big day arrived, I felt myself getting more nervous by the minute. Every worst-case scenario went through my head. Would I be attacked? What about diseases? I had read everything I could about STDs, but I was still worried. What would I tell my wife? What was

I doing? Finally, I decided that I wanted to cancel the meeting. I was just too nervous.

I texted Josh, "I'm really nervous. I don't think I'm ready for this. I hope you understand."

Within minutes, Josh responded. He told me that it was okay and reminded me that we weren't going to do anything anyway.

That put me somewhat at ease. I told him that I would come over, just to say hi. I don't know if I really believed that, but I wanted to put myself in a position where it would be possible to have an experience. I was okay with this scenario as long as I had a way out—even if it was just an imaginary exit route.

"I'm going out!" I called to Michelle as I left the house. By that point, our relationship was strained enough that she didn't even ask where I was going.

I left thirty minutes before our meeting, even though the guy's house was only fifteen minutes away. I needed to scope out the area. His house looked like a normal bungalow set in a suburban neighbourhood. There was nothing special or threatening about it. I don't know what I was looking for. Any reason not to go, I suppose. Something that would raise a red flag. But there was nothing. I parked my car down the road so he couldn't connect me to it or write down my licence plate number. Paranoia can take you to some interesting places.

I spent a long ten minutes looking at the quiet street from the driver's seat of my car. A guy walking his dog passed me, and I tried to look invisible. Nine minutes passed. I breathed in deeply, held my breath, and then exhaled. *I'm going to do this*, I thought. After all, I could always just leave if I wanted to. I reminded myself that I was six feet tall and, yes, skinny, but also stronger than I looked. I could get out of a messy situation if I had to.

I got out of the car and walked down the street. I wondered if Josh lived with someone. I would have thought that only families lived in this area and in this type of house. I walked up to the front door and took another deep breath. The night was chilly, and I noticed a cloud of warm steam exiting my mouth. I found the doorbell and reached out to press it. *Wait. Should I knock or use the doorbell?* I decided to use the doorbell. After all, it was there for a reason, and I didn't want to stand out there any longer than I had to. I heard the bell ring on the other side of the door.

The door opened, and there he was, live and in person. Josh smiled at me and scanned me quickly from top to bottom. Despite my nerves, I managed to check him out as well. (Maybe I was more ready for this than I thought, since I appeared to have the ability to check a guy out in an instant.) I had seen his photo on the app and knew what to expect, but of course, photos are easily manipulated, and we all know our best angles. Standing in front of me, as advertised, was a handsome, fit, Asian guy. I was definitely interested in finding out more about him. Then I started to worry that he might be disappointed in me.

Apparently not. Josh nudged the door opened a little wider and gestured for me to enter. I responded to the gesture as if I were being pulled into the house. All I said was hello as I peeked inside to see if anyone else was there or if there was anything in the house that might make me want to bolt. But no. It was just a normal house, and I could see that he lived by himself.

Once I finished scanning the house for potential threats, I shifted my attention to Josh.

He walked to the sofa and gestured for me to join him. Obediently, I sat down on the cushion he'd pointed to. From the other end of the sofa where he sat, Josh turned off the video game he'd been playing and turned on a music channel. He offered me a beer, which I accepted with relief. I needed something to help me calm down.

I finished the beer fairly quickly as we chatted. Josh asked how I was doing and what I was going through. I didn't share *all* the details, but I told him enough. Josh understood that I was exploring my sexuality and had never been with a man before. I told Josh that I had kids, but I wasn't so honest about my marriage. I said I was separated. By that point, it didn't feel far from the truth. Josh listened carefully and without judgment, which made me feel at ease.

It was interesting to feel a different dynamic at play in our interaction than I had ever experienced. I was always the one in control in my relationship with Michelle. But in this moment, I felt as if Josh was taking control and I was being happily led. I really liked that feeling. As time has gone on, I've come to realize that one of the things I enjoy most about gay relationships is the fluidity they offer and the lack of rigid gender roles.

Josh and I talked some more, and then he began to make his move.

It turns out that I was very coachable, and things moved faster than I had anticipated. Don't get me wrong: I was a willing participant. Despite the fact that this experience was a first for me, I felt comfortable and safe. There was passion, and I could feel myself losing track of time and everything else around me. We moved to the bedroom, and it felt as if my body had been waiting for this my entire life. A sense of happiness and complete pleasure rushed over me in a way I'd never experienced before. I wasn't thinking anymore; I was completely in the moment. I knew beyond a shadow of a doubt that I was exactly where I should be.

When all was said and done, Josh seemed happy with the experience too. We parted ways with a hug. I never imagined that I could feel such intimacy with a person I had just met, yet here it was. As the door closed and I walked back to the car, I felt as if I was walking on a cloud. I was consumed by a feeling of wholeness and happiness not only within but also without. *The world is perfect,* I thought. *And everything is just as it should be!*

Later, after I came out, my friends all assumed that my sex life with Michelle must have been horrible for all those years. But that wasn't the case. I really loved Michelle, and the sex was good. It wasn't until I experienced sex with a man that I realized there was an entirely different level of experience available to me, a more complete one, where I could lose myself.

As I walked back to my car, I realized that I no longer cared if anyone saw me. As I opened the door and sat down, I knew once and for all: I was gay. There were no more doubts or excuses. I knew! It felt so good, as if I had finally found my identity. It wasn't the sex that was sending me into this state of euphoria. It was the feeling of acceptance and the understanding that I had finally shed light on a large part of who I was. For the first time in my life, I didn't care what people thought of me. I was no longer in the dark, and in fact, I could now be a source of light. I could let my own light shine from this day forward. *This is what being free and alive feels like!* I thought.

Of course, that night wasn't really the *first* time I'd ever felt alive. I'd felt it in small moments before, like after drinking a good cup of coffee on an empty stomach, when warmth, energy, and caffeine radiate through my body. It's that feeling of physical and mental satisfaction after you eat your favourite meal or snack, free of guilt.

I had felt alive any time I'd committed myself to doing something hard or scary. That rush feels a lot like taking a ride at the amusement park. The excitement of strapping in. The lurch as the car starts moving forward and then, slowly but surely, begins ascending. The small knot that forms in my stomach as the horizon grows bigger and closer and the amusement park takes on a different perspective from above. Of course, I know that at some point this slow pace upward will stop and turn into a free fall. The cart slows down in that moment before it drops and adrenaline pumps through my body. All my senses are at full awareness; I am equally scared and excited.

In those moments when I feel alive, there is a feeling of connectivity with and love for everything that exists. Everything else falls away, and for just a moment, all in the universe is perfect.

I experienced that same feeling as I left Josh's house. Finally, I knew who I was. Everything felt so right. My entire world had been rocked, and it had been so much more than just a physical experience.

As I sat in the car, my mind flipped through other moments in my past when I had felt this alive, this feeling of connectivity. I remembered a random spring day, when I stood in front of our house as all three kids were playing outside. It was close to winter but still felt great to be outside. The two boys were playing basketball while my daughter sprawled on the ground, drawing intently. I was several feet away, looking at them with the house in the background. Out of nowhere, I was suddenly overtaken by a massive wave of love—for my children, for the world. Everything was perfect in that moment.

And then, just like that moment of perfection in the front yard with my children passed, so did that moment in my car outside of Josh's house. In its place was a deep-seated fear that became stronger by the minute.

Now that I knew, I had to tell Michelle.

CHAPTER FOURTEEN

A Long Three Months

Suddenly, there were no more questions to be asked, no more need for exploration. There was no need for me to bury the truth for the sake of my marriage or my love for my wife, which I still very much felt, even though our relationship had been strained for a long time.

My next meeting with Derek was scheduled for two days after my experience with Josh. I walked up the stairs to his small office like I always did. I knocked on the door and made my way to the same couch I always sat on.

Derek and I sat across from one another in silence. I waited for him to talk first, as if I was somehow playing an unspoken game. Of course, Derek didn't know we were playing a game. He didn't know that today was anything other than a regular day. It dawned on me that our last meeting hadn't been the watershed moment in his life that it had been in mine.

"So, how are you doing today, Alon?" he asked at last.

I looked up at the ceiling. Suddenly I had doubts. Was I *really* gay? Maybe I had just enjoyed a physical experience. Wasn't that possible? Nonetheless, I began telling Derek what had happened. As I spoke, I relived the experience. I could hear my own voice get more energetic and more emotional, almost as if I were witnessing someone else speaking.

Derek listened as I let it all out. When I finished, he asked the same question I had been asking myself over and over again for the past forty-eight hours: "What now?"

Those words felt almost as if they had a physical impact on me, and I descended into fear and darkness. "Well, now I have to tell my wife," I heard myself say again.

Outside of fear, I didn't feel much. There was no room for emotion in this moment. I knew there was no other option, nothing left to do or resolve before I told Michelle. It was as if I was playing a game and had used up all the other options except for the final move that I really didn't want to make. As far as I knew, choosing this particular option would change my world entirely. The next course of action was clear, but nothing else was. On the one hand, after four decades of life, I had finally aligned with my true self. On the other hand, my family's future seemed uncertain and bleak as a result.

Derek smiled at me. "Alon," he said with great assurance, "you will be okay. Go and do what you need to do. Call me if you want to talk."

After leaving Derek's office, I made my way to a nearby restaurant and sat down at a corner table. I needed to be by myself in that moment. I was terrified at the thought of telling Michelle about my realization, which would change everything for her just as much as for me. How would she respond? Would this end up like one of those disastrous breakups I'd heard about at Gay Fathers of Toronto?

I ran through several what-if scenarios. I thought about how different coming out would be if I didn't have kids or a wife. I wondered how I would fare in the gay community. Would I ever even find anyone after all this? I thought that I was probably destined to be alone, with no partner, an angry ex-wife, and kids who wouldn't want to see me.

But even as all that negativity was swirling through my mind, I still knew that I had to come out. *This is who I am, and this is what I need to do,* I told myself. I refused to let an unwritten future dictate my decisions. If I was destined to be alone, then so be it.

Michelle had to be the first person to know. Everyone else would come after. Now I just needed to find the right moment to tell her. The right moment to shatter the world we'd built into a million little pieces.

I left that corner table and drove back to work with those thoughts still swirling in my head. I put on a show of normality. Little did the people around me know what was just under the surface, ready to emerge and disrupt everything in unknown ways. Thank God for routine. No more than an hour later, work pulled me in, and I almost forgot about everything that lay ahead. It wasn't until it was almost time to go home that the thoughts and worries pushed their way to the front of my mind.

As I drove home, I worried that I somehow looked different than I had before. I arrived, greeted the kids, and avoided Michelle by making myself busy with other things. Really, it wasn't that much different than any other weeknight over the past couple of years. Except that it was because now I knew who I was, and I knew what was coming.

It used to take me forever to get into a swimming pool. First, I would look at the water from the ledge of the pool. Then, after a while, I would dip my toes in. Eventually, slowly but surely, I would make my way into the pool, one inch at a time. Waiting to find that perfect moment to tell Michelle the news felt a lot like that.

I spent a lot of time lying awake at night, staring into the dark and wondering what that perfect moment looked like. Did it even exist? When exactly *is* the right time to tell your wife of eighteen years that the reality she knows is not actually reality after all? It felt as if I had been given control over the exact moment of the death of our relationship, the moment I pulled the plug. By this point, there wasn't much life left in the relationship, but the vital signs were still there.

Life continued as normal while I waited three long months, searching for that elusive moment. During that time, I only became more certain about who I was.

Then one night, my parents took the kids for a sleepover. It was a rare occurrence for all three of them to be there at the same time. That evening, Michelle and I were invited to go out with a few friends, two of whom happened to be a gay couple. Despite all the tension at home, every once in a while, Michelle and I still went out with friends. By this point, we were well practiced in the art of acting normal. The evening went well. I drank and talked and drank some more.

As Michelle and I were in the car on the way home, I realized that this was the night. The moment had arrived. The gay couple had set the energy for the evening, and the alcohol had helped. These circumstances were the best I could hope for. The minutes ticked by, every second bringing me closer to the moment when everything would change.

Finally, I turned to Michelle, who was driving because I'd had too much to drink, and said, "I'd like to talk to you once we get home."

For many months, Michelle had given me the space I needed. She was very good at giving space, and I was good at taking it.

The silence between us had lingered since that day six months before when I'd had a meltdown in the car. The only time we'd discussed our relationship in the ensuing months was when I told her that I was going to see a therapist. My guess is that she was hoping I was doing some work on myself to salvage our relationship. Michelle was all about family. Me and the kids were the most important part of her life. That was one of the reasons I was so afraid to talk to her. I didn't want to demolish Michelle's dream life, even though it surely wasn't much of a dream these days.

The closer we got to home, the more the alcohol started to wear off. When we arrived home, Michelle parked the car, and we walked into the house. I was careful not to make eye contact. I felt my stress levels increasing. It was as if I was on that roller coaster, moving up, up, up to the highest point, with the anticipation and fear of the free fall building up inside of me. There was no getting off the ride this time. I couldn't back out. Everything had led us to this moment, and I simultaneously felt certain and fearful.

A light sweat built up as I opened the door and we walked up the few stairs to our living room. I excused myself to go to the washroom. As the door closed behind me, I lifted both of my hands above my head to allow more air into my lungs. I leaned against the wall and concentrated on breathing in and out, in and out. Finally, I thought, *Here goes nothing.* I flushed the toilet to keep up the façade that I had used it. I don't know why I did that. Perhaps covering up had become a force of habit by then. Soon, I wouldn't need to do that anymore.

I arrived in the living room to find Michelle sitting on our brown sofa. She looked up at me as I entered the room, and I could feel her gaze continue to follow me as I sat down. I was careful not to make eye contact in return.

I sat down in the chair across from the sofa, farthest away from where Michelle sat. The coffee table was between us.

I knew Michelle was ready for something big; the energy in the room felt dark and somber.

There was still no eye contact as I began speaking. "So you remember that I began going to a therapist a couple of months ago?" I started. I lifted my eyes to glance at her.

Michelle nodded. Was that hope I saw in her eyes? I needed to end this nightmare now.

"Well, the therapist I'm seeing helps people with sexuality issues." *Don't stop now!* I told myself. "The reason couples therapy didn't help us, and we just got frustrated? Well, the issue is with me. I am gay."

This was only the second time I had used that word to describe myself out loud. It was hard to say. I could *think* it, but saying it was something else entirely.

As I talked, my tears began to flow. "It was always part of me. When we met and got married, I loved you and was attracted to you. I still love you, but a few years ago, this frustration began emerging within me." At this point, I broke eye contact with Michelle. I needed to finish saying what I had to say before I could look directly at her. "And it slowly came to the surface. I can't ignore it any longer. I had never cheated on you, but three months ago, the therapist suggested that I needed to find out. So I did. And I am." I explained to Michelle that, until a few weeks ago, I had only thought about being with a man and even thought that I might be bisexual. But now I knew, and so she had to know too.

"I can't imagine living away from you and the kids," I finished. The tears were flowing out of my eyes by this point. I lifted my head up to look at Michelle. She was crying too.

Michelle talked, but I don't remember what she said. I was too overwhelmed and emotional. I know that I was sitting on the floor. I know that I kept saying I was sorry. I know that it was the end.

CHAPTER FIFTEEN

> Hello, World

That night after the Big Reveal, I slept well—especially considering the fact that everything in my life was uncertain now. Where would I live? What would everyone say? Who would stop talking to me? What would my parents do? Would I ever find a partner?

And yet I felt lighter. There was no turning back now, and that felt good.

The next morning, I woke up and walked up to the kitchen. Michelle looked terrible. It was obvious that she hadn't slept much. I felt so bad.

We greeted each other. Even though we had known each other for so long, we both seemed different.

I felt so bad for Michelle. I had suffered for many years, and sure, I might have more suffering ahead of me. But she was just embarking upon a new, unforeseen path of suffering. I wished I could spare her, but I knew that I could not, so I was ready to follow her lead. At that point, her needs were more important than mine. She needed support. I took some comfort in the fact that Michelle had a good group of friends and people in her life who loved her.

That day at work, I felt as if I were wearing a mask when I interacted with people. Everything was the same, and yet it wasn't. All I could think about was the conversation Michelle and I would have that evening. For me, the hard part was done, but now we needed to clean up the mess I'd made and plan for the future.

When I got home, the mask was still on. We dealt with the kids' afternoon routine like we always did. *Do they notice anything?* I wondered. There was a bleak energy in the air, but I guess they were used to it by this point.

Michelle and I did all we could in that strange, in-between moment in time, when everything about our lives still appeared the way it always had before. We focussed on the kids. They were in their early teens. All I wanted to do was to wrap them in a bubble and keep them safe. But, of course, that's not how it works.

It was late November at this point, and our oldest son would turn thirteen in January. This meant that it was time for his bar mitzvah. It was a big deal for him, and we had planned on going to visit our family in Israel to celebrate the special occasion.

We decided to wait until after we had celebrated our son's bar mitzvah to tell anyone. We didn't want his special day to be tainted in any way.

Since our trip to Israel wasn't until April, that meant maintaining the appearance of normalcy for about six more months. I could do that.

I was in awe of what a good mother Michelle was. Her world had just been turned upside down, and her first thought was the kids.

I assured Michelle that we didn't need to make all the decisions about the future right away. We could take it slow. And I promised her that the kids would always come first.

We agreed that I would move out of the house once we returned from Israel.

I told Michelle that I knew this changed everything, but that I still loved and cared for her, and I wouldn't do anything to hurt her or the kids. We would talk everything through before we made any decisions.

Waiting until May to move struck me as a good thing. It gave us time to figure out our next steps in a thoughtful way. And it was also immediately clear that there weren't going to be any wars. I was relieved.

So life continued as it had before.

In some ways, it wasn't ideal to remain in limbo for several months, but it did give both of us time to process our new reality.

For me, there was also a sense of relief. The two biggest obstacles that had loomed over me for so long now were behind me: coming out to myself and then to my wife.

We carried on as normal. It wasn't as if this show was new to us. For all intents and purposes, we had been apart for some time now, and it seemed as if we had both adapted to our somewhat robotic roles.

But inside, I was getting excited. I couldn't wait to start my new life.

I had a small list of people close to me who Michelle and I agreed I could entrust with my secret before we told the kids. This included my parents, brothers, and a handful of friends. And there was my next steep mountain to climb: how was I supposed to tell people who had always known me as straight that I was actually gay? They all knew me in a certain way, in a certain context. How would this new piece of information affect my relationships? I thought about how I might feel if someone delivered this sort of news to me. The truth is, I didn't know how I would react if I thought I knew someone only to find out that there was an entire aspect of them that I was completely unaware of.

When I think about it today, I suppose there are two approaches to coming out. The first is to rip the Band-Aid off and get it over with quickly. That way, all the gossip, shock, and judgment happens in a short period of time, and then it's done with. If I were young, I think I would have chosen that option. But those were not my circumstances. I had a lot of baggage and complexity to contend with. Also, it was all so new for me that I needed to go slow. So I decided my approach would be to tear off the Band-Aid slowly and tell one person at a time. There was no rush. After all, I had six months.

I decided to tell one of my best friends first. We were kindred spirits. He was much younger than me, but we really got each other. He was also a very nonjudgmental person.

We met at a bar that another one of our mutual friends owned. The bar was lit in such a way that most people looked attractive even before their first drink. I always felt cooler just because I was sitting in that bar.

That night, I arrived early. My strategy was to have a couple of beers before delivering my news. The first beer went down quickly. I decided to drink the second one more slowly. I wanted to be tipsy, but I also wanted to keep my wits about me so that I could accurately gauge how my friend was responding. That strategy didn't work. I was on my third beer by the time he got there, just before eight.

I waved him over, and he approached with a smile. He wasn't aware that I had a life-changing message to share. As far as he was concerned, we were just hanging out like we normally did.

My friend ordered a drink, and we started chatting. I told him that I wanted to tell him something, but kept delaying delivering my message. As the alcohol took effect, I relaxed, and eventually, I told him.

I will never forget his response. He reacted as if I had just told him that it was going to rain tomorrow. Then, he followed up with a few questions about how I had arrived at this point. I filled him in on everything, and when I finished, he got up and gave me a hug.

"I'm happy for you," he said, looking me dead in the eyes. It was clear that he was.

Years later, writing about this experience still makes me emotional. It was such a critical moment for me. It showed me that the friends who accepted me for who I was would be happy for me. It also showed me that if someone's response was negative—well, that was okay too. Maybe our paths would just diverge from there.

I was still extremely nervous, but I was ready to accept whatever consequences might come my way as a result of coming out.

Of course, one of the people I felt it was most important to come out to was my mom.

My mom had painted for her entire life. A few years before I came out, she took over an office located right next to mine and converted it into a studio. She spent a few hours there almost every day. It was so nice to see her walk by, to start the day hearing, "Good morning, Alon!" in her English accent. The proximity brought us closer. On her breaks, my mom would often come over to my office and chat. She usually stood as we talked because she didn't like to sit down much. She was always on the move: going out for a walk, swimming at the local pool, or doing tai chi a couple of times per week. Sometimes we went out for lunch together.

Several times while we were talking, I wondered, *Should I tell her now?* Every time, I decided not to. We had a very good relationship, and I was certain of her love for me. She was always asking me how I felt. On days when my head hurt, she would sit me down on a chair and stand behind me, slowly and lovingly massaging my head. She had such good energy; without fail, the pain and pressure would disappear within minutes. I think the fact that she loved me so much also helped the healing.

My mom loved my children very much too. She would do anything for them. She was one of those grandmothers who allowed her grandchildren to get away with anything, and she also constantly worried about their well-being. That was the reason I held back from telling her my news.

I knew she would worry for her grandchildren and go into overdrive to protect them as soon as she found out.

I loved my mom very much. When we were together, just the two of us, our dynamic was always nice and chill. But when the kids were in the room, she became a different person. There was an air of nervousness about her, and everyone else aside from the grandchildren was rendered to a second-rate position. She was too busy worrying about all the different ways the kids might get hurt and, in turn, what she could do to protect them. Many times, this involved telling Michelle and me how we should take care of our kids. To be honest, when my mom was in the same room as the kids, I often had to excuse myself. I didn't like her stressful energy. But when it was just her and the kids, they enjoyed a beautiful rhythm together. They did arts and crafts and spent time outside. She was an amazing grandmother, and she truly enriched their lives.

All of this held me back. I found myself constantly waiting for a window of opportunity to tell my mom.

One day in early December, my dad called around nine looking for Mom. I told him that I hadn't seen her. There was nothing strange about that because she usually didn't come to paint that early.

Then my dad told me that her car was in the driveway.

"Well, then, she's probably just walking around the block as she often does," I replied.

My dad agreed and told me that he had a dentist appointment soon.

I went back to work without giving any of this a second thought. Around noon, my dad called me again. "Alon,

Mom isn't home, but her car is still in the driveway. Do you know where she is?"

I assumed she had come back from her walk and headed out to go shopping. "Did you look around the house for her?" I asked.

He told me he did.

"Did you check her room?"

My parents slept in separate bedrooms because my father's snoring ranks high on the Richter Scale.

When my dad said that he hadn't checked her room, I felt myself start to get nervous. "Dad, go check her room, and keep the phone with you."

So he walked up the five stairs to my mom's room. I heard him open the door and immediately gasp and then wail, "Oh, my God! She's gone! She is gone!"

I understood immediately what he was saying.

My mom had died of a massive heart attack on her way to the washroom in the early morning hours. The coroner said that she was probably dead before her body hit the ground.

I never got the chance to come out to my mom. Today I joke with friends that it was probably better that I didn't. What if I had told her I was gay and she'd dropped dead the next day? Everyone would have blamed me! In all seriousness, I wasn't afraid that she would have had a heart attack or disowned me, as some more traditional parents might. I knew that our connection was too strong for that. Mom and I would have gotten along just fine. It was her concern for the family as a whole that I had needed more time to prepare for. I've wondered if, deep down inside, she knew that I was gay. The truth is, I'm not sure. Looking back, there were signs, but they were subtle.

I came out to my brothers a few months before we told the kids. I was confident that my conversations with both of them would go well. Guy and Aharon both had good friends who were gay, and sexuality wasn't an issue for them.

Guy is logical and a leader. One day, I found myself at work with a couple of hours free. As I sat in my chair, staring out the window at the snow that had fallen the night before, I suddenly knew that I was ready to tell Guy. I wanted him to be one of the first people to know. I knew that he would support me and watch my back as I came out to others and word spread.

I took a deep breath and yelled through the wall, "Guy, when you have a minute, can you please come over? I have something I want to tell you."

"Sure. Let me just finish something first," he yelled back.

Even though I knew he would be okay, I started to get nervous.

A couple of minutes later, I heard Guy's chair slide back and his door open. He entered my office and nodded at me. Even though there was a chair, he kept standing.

Good, I thought to myself. *I will tell him, and then he will leave.* I figured we didn't need to have a long, drawn-out conversation.

"What's up, Alon?" he prompted me.

"I have something to tell you," I began.

As I delivered the news, he didn't so much as flinch. When I finished, Guy just looked at me and said, "Okay. I'm happy for you. The kids will be okay, and so will Michelle." He then asked me a couple of questions about logistics, and within a few minutes, he started talking about business as usual.

Very quickly, I got the coming-out process down to a science. I still needed to gather up my courage before each conversation, but I developed a structure for the conversation that went like this:

I have something to tell you.

When I married Michelle, I loved her and was attracted to her.

I always felt a little different from everyone else.

As time passed, I felt this feeling rise inside me until I couldn't ignore it anymore.

My relationship with Michelle suffered.

I had never been with a man before.

Once I tried it, I knew I was gay.

My wife and I are good with each other.

The kids come first.

Obviously, some of my loved ones had questions beyond this, and when they did, I tried to answer as truthfully as possible. But those questions usually came later, after they'd had a chance to process this new situation.

When I was ready to tell my dad, he was in Israel. I didn't want to wait, so I made sure my brother Aharon (who already knew) was with him. I also wanted to make sure an ambulance was accessible nearby. When I told my brother that, half joking and half not, he said I might be overreacting.

My dad is the nicest man. He loves people as they are and rarely judges them. He offers friendship unconditionally to all. The reason I was worried is because on some occasions when sexuality had come up in conversation, my dad commented that he could not understand how people could be gay. He never said this with any sort of anger or judgment; it was just that he didn't get it. When gay friends visited our household, he always treated them just the same as he did everyone else, and there was never any commentary about them. I just wasn't sure how he would react to the news that his son was gay.

I told my dad that I wanted to tell him something, but first I wanted him to read an email that I was going to send him soon. I wanted to give him some time to wrap his mind around the information and come up with any questions he might have before we spoke. After sending the email, I checked in with my brother to make sure dad received it. My brother confirmed that my dad had read the email.

Then I called.

I was a bit worried about the fact that my dad is from a generation that doesn't show emotion. How would I know what he really thought? I kept thinking back to the gay pride parade that used to pass by our first store at Yonge and Wellesley Streets in downtown Toronto. The first year the shop was open, the guys came into our store from the parade, happy and touchy. I will never forget the moment my dad witnessed his first gay kiss. Or rather, he *didn't* see it because he turned away. He wasn't hateful or angry about it. It was just that his eyes were not used to such a sight. It was a lot for him to take in.

The next year, we stocked up on water and set up a point of sale just outside the store. My dad stood out there, moving his body ever so slightly to the music blaring from the floats as they drove by. I guess his eyes were used to the sight of men kissing by then.

When I called Dad, my brother picked up the phone. "How did he take it?" I asked.

"He's okay," my brother replied. "A little surprised, but he'll be okay." I was relieved to hear an ambulance hadn't been necessary after all. With that, my brother handed the phone to my dad.

"Did you read the email?" I asked when my dad got on the line.

"Yes, I did."

"So I am gay. Everything is okay. Michelle and I are both caring for the kids."

"Okay," he replied.

And that was that.

From there on out, my dad was always supportive of me. I know that it was initially hard for him to see me with my partners, but he was always welcoming and warm to us. I appreciate him so much for that. In fact, I'm tearing up as I think back on it.

Today, his eyes are used to seeing me with another man.

CHAPTER SIXTEEN

Grounded and Free

As I began to shed the shackles I'd worn for so long, I began to feel a new sense of freedom that came from being comfortable in my own skin.

What I find odd is that early on in life, I didn't feel these shackles. It's as if, back then, I didn't know what I didn't know. It's not that I wasn't wearing the shackles. It's just that they were self-imposed, and I was so used to them from such a young age that they seemed normal to me. I didn't notice their weight or the way they constricted me. It was only when the truth about who I really was began to rise to the surface that I began to feel the weight I had been carrying around on a daily basis.

With time, I began to understand the price that both my loved ones and me had paid for those shackles. I had trained and brainwashed myself about who I "needed" to be for so long that I was able to ignore the signs about my sexuality that were there from the very beginning. I was only able to ultimately acknowledge it out loud and in a meaningful way because my therapist said I owed it to Michelle. I was unable to do that for myself. I think this is a testament to my great love for and commitment to Michelle (even during that time when our relationship was so broken) and the lack of love I felt for myself in those days.

I quickly found that the more I accepted myself, the freer I felt. At first, this acceptance and ensuing freedom came in small drops. I made small admissions in my head, one at a time. Those thoughts became reality, and my sense of freedom grew.

This gave me a new sense of grounding. I came to realize that I had been living my life up to that point like a tree that was mostly uprooted. I couldn't get all the nutrients I needed from the soil, so I couldn't grow to my full potential. The water was sparse, so I was less resilient. I felt small and weak. External forces like the wind could sway me and potentially uproot me. Over time, I suppose that all that wear and tear against such weak defences could have led to my demise.

Through this, I think I seemed okay enough from the outside, but inside, I was a mess. My relationship was collapsing, and I lived in a constant state of stress, depression, and sadness. All of it affected me more and got worse as I continued to ignore who I was and that I felt uprooted.

As I began accepting who I was, I sensed new possibility in my life. From the moment of that first physical experience with Josh, it was as if a new connection to the universe had revealed itself to me, and my energy began to flow in a different way.

In those in-between months after I came out to Michelle but before we told the kids, I had to take a short business trip to Montreal. I decided to invite a guy with me. We had been meeting up once in a while. It was nothing serious, but we enjoyed each other's company and had a fun physical relationship. I booked us a romantic hotel set in the heart of old Montreal. I upgraded us to a room with cool antique furniture and a fireplace. I would never have spent that much on a room for business, but this time, there was pleasure involved too, so I did.

My date and I agreed that I would pick him up from the subway station at eight, and we would head out on the five-hour road trip to Montreal from there. Excited, I drove down Yonge Street towards the station that was located just before the highway leading out of the city. He was standing there with his backpack on when I arrived. I waved, and he hopped into the car, threw his bag in the backseat, and he kissed me. I kissed him back.

That was the first time I had kissed another man in public—and really, it's not something that I engaged in until a bit further down the road. Even today, I don't feel comfortable kissing a man in a heterosexual environment or in front of my kids. But on that particular day, I was so excited that I couldn't resist. At that point, I was still afraid of being seen by people who knew me since I wasn't really out yet, except to a small circle of family and close friends.

We started driving towards Montreal. I turned on the radio and enjoyed the comfortable energy in the car. It felt so right. Halfway through the drive, we stopped to fuel up the car and get some coffee in rural Ontario. Most of the customers there were from a little town just off the highway. As the two of us walked in to get our coffee, I noticed a few glances drifting in our direction. We weren't holding hands or anything, but I could tell that some of these people knew we were together, which would have freaked me out completely back home. But here, it felt so good to be seen for who and what I authentically was that I moved closer to my date so that our shoulders touched. It was my way of signalling, "No, we are not just friends."

By the time we returned to the car, my heart was pumping wildly. I felt so alive! I reached over and grabbed his hand. We continued holding hands all the way from that coffee shop until we got to Montreal a couple of hours later. The world felt perfect.

I wasn't in love. I was having fun with a person I liked. This feeling of perfection wasn't coming from the fact that I was blinded by love. It was because my mind felt quiet and still. It was a wonderful break for someone like me, whose mind was always going, who was always worrying about something somewhere in the background. But not now. During this drive, all I felt was complete peace. Prior to this point in my life, the only time I recall my mind letting go of worry is when I was a young child and excitement would take over when I was allowed to have chocolate on Fridays. Or in anticipation of my birthday and the present I might receive from my parents. Or the excitement before Purim, the Jewish version of Halloween, and the thrill of getting to dress up as a prince and wear my favourite shiny shoes. (See? I told you there were *some* signs all along!)

We made our way through the old stone-paved roads of Montreal and drove up to the hotel, where a valet, a young guy with a French accent, was waiting. I handed him the car key, and we made our way to reception. As we reached the counter and the person at the front desk looked up at us, the old me got stressed out for a second. *Don't assume that we're together!* I thought defensively. *Maybe we're just friends visiting this romantic city and staying in an upgraded room with a fireplace.* I caught myself at that moment and realized that we were not back home, and nobody knew us here. I think that the difference between my reaction to being seen as part of a gay couple was different here at the hotel than it had been at the coffee shop because I perceived the hotel stay to be associated with sex, whereas more everyday encounters were not. Unfortunately, there is a degree of shame associated with the physical aspect of being gay for men. Or at least there was for me.

The girl at the front desk went over the details of our room—one bed, a fireplace, and two keys, correct?

"Yes, yes," I said, rushing her along. "That's our room. Thank you."

She handed us the room keys with the glint of a smile in her eyes. "Enjoy, guys!"

Any stress I felt at the front desk disappeared as we walked towards the elevator. I felt as if I was on my honeymoon. A honeymoon with the new me. From that moment on, I was free!

A few weeks before, I had booked us a seven o'clock reservation at a trendy new restaurant that I really wanted to try. It was located in the trendy Plato area of the city. We walked through the busy streets to dinner holding hands. When we arrived, the restaurant was packed. It was dimly lit to create an intimate atmosphere, a vibe that always makes me want to be inside with the cool people.

As we were escorted to our table, I scanned the restaurant and noticed that we were the only gay couple there. A few people looked up as we walked by. This was a new experience for me. I wasn't used to being noticed as I entered places. It would have killed me back home in Toronto, but I must say that I enjoyed the feeling of being noticed here, away from my real life. Just as I had at the coffee shop, I again walked closer to my date to make sure everyone knew that we were together.

We had such a good time that, before long, I stopped noticing the stares.

Maybe we were old news by then, or maybe their attention had all been in my mind to begin with.

CHAPTER SEVENTEEN

New Life, New Home

A month or so before I came out to my kids, I decided to start looking for an apartment. The suburb where Michelle and I lived consisted entirely of private homes, but there were a few ugly brick apartment buildings that were built in the 1960s within a ten-minute drive. I decided to start there. As much as I didn't like the buildings, it made sense for me to check them out due to their proximity and affordable price.

I planned to find a two-bedroom so I would have room for the kids to stay over every other weekend. In addition to that, Michelle and I had agreed that I would visit them a couple of times per week at the house.

There were many realtors in our circle of friends, but I wasn't ready for the word to get out yet, so I contacted a random real estate agent named Boris. Boris was an older gentleman who immediately assumed that I was freshly divorced. He told me he knew exactly what I was looking for: a sensible living solution close to my kids. I confirmed that he was correct. By that point in my life, I had a long-established track record of making reasonable, logical decisions.

I was excited to see the apartments and find my new home as a new person. Boris and I agreed to meet at the mall next to the apartment buildings. It was a chilly yet sunny day in early spring. I parked and found Boris nearby, waiting for me in a Mercedes SUV. It seems that all real estate agents drive luxury vehicles, I imagine as a marketing tool.

"Hello, Alon," he called out in his Russian accent. "You will love it here!"

Boris began our tour by showing me the suburban area around the building. I noticed that the building seemed to get uglier the nearer we got. I blocked that thought out, hoping the units would be large and full of light. Who cared what they looked like from the outside, right? We approached the main entrance, entered the lobby, and took the elevator up. The hallway smelled like cabbage soup. I'm sure there were other smells too, but the scent of soup was overpowering. I was now hopeful that the apartment would compensate not just for the exterior of the building but for the smell in the corridor as well.

Boris dug into his pocket and extracted a key. He opened the door, and we entered a very average-looking apartment. As promised, it had two bedrooms and a reasonable living room. It looked fine, but I felt as if reality had delivered me a punch in the gut. I couldn't imagine starting a new phase of my life *here*.

I hid my reaction from Boris. As we looked around, he made a few comments about how lucky I was to be divorced because now I could get lots of young ladies. I didn't correct Boris, but his take on the situation made me smile inside.

We looked at three buildings in the area, and they all looked the same. I felt depressed and decided to stop my search for the time being.

A week before our talk with the kids, I was lying in my bed in the basement, feeling my levels of stress increase over the fact that I still didn't have a place to move into. I figured I would have to be practical and just rent one of the places I had seen with Boris. But as I pondered the thought, I heard a small voice in my head say, *Fuck that.* I decided to look at other options.

The following day, I decided to change up two things. The first was my real estate agent. Instead of Boris, I decided to work with an agent I had met through a good friend of mine. She was younger and knew my story. The second was the area. I wanted to target a more expensive neighbourhood that had newer buildings. It was five minutes farther from our family home and located on a subway line that would give me direct access to the downtown life I craved so much. The agent and I met for coffee in a bustling area near the subway station. She asked me if I wanted to buy or rent. I told her that I couldn't afford to buy, so a rental it was.

The next day, we met again, this time to check out a few units. The buildings were much newer and felt so much better than the ones I had seen with Boris. The views were great, and the corridors did not smell of soup. In one building, the agent took me through an apartment that was for sale just to see it. It was a small two-bedroom on the twenty-fifth floor with beautiful city views. Despite its size, it felt right. *I could live here*, I thought.

But, of course, it was for sale, and I didn't have the money for a down payment.

Down in the basement that night, I thought about the predicament I was in. And then, out of the blue, I thought of my good friend Harry. He always looked like a GQ model. Not only did he have the looks; he also had style. No matter what his financial situation, at any given moment, Harry always looked like a million bucks. In that moment, I decided to be like Harry. I deserved that apartment, and I would make it happen.

That was the first time in my life I'd ever had a thought like that. Up to that point, I had always been realistic and reasonable when it came to my personal choices. This was in contrast to how I was in business, where I never accepted reality and always strived for more. It was thanks to this quality that I was able to start a small business and build it into a fairly large one against all odds.

Interestingly, coming out brought with it a new degree of "selfishness." For the first time, I realized that I was important and that it was okay to want things just because I wanted them. Up until this point, I had spent so much of my life doing what I thought other people thought I should do.

I wanted that apartment. It felt like the right place to start this new life of mine.

The next day, I spoke with my brother and dad. I told them that I needed a loan for the down payment. The old me would have felt very uncomfortable doing that. But the new me was good with asking. What was the worst that could happen? They might say no, but that was okay.

Within two days, they agreed.

Within the week, I got the apartment.

A few weeks later, I moved in.

I was truly excited to be there. The place had great energy, and even though the second room was small, it managed to fit three beds for the kids. Sure, you couldn't see any floor, but it was cozy and warm.

Buying an apartment that excited me rather than renting a reasonable apartment in the suburbs that smelled like soup changed something in me.

Selfishness kicked in again when I bought new furniture. In the past I had always bought furniture because it fit in with the rest of the house or offered a good payment plan. This time, I approached the process in a different way entirely. I went to stores that felt good to me. I bought furniture that made me feel good. I still have most of that furniture today. Even though I paid more than I would have previously, I found that the furniture lasted longer. It was an investment in myself, my home, and my future.

I spent more upfront and saved in the long run.

CHAPTER EIGHTEEN

Telling the Kids

April rolled around, and as planned, we travelled to Israel as a family to celebrate my son's bar mitzvah. Technically, Michelle and I were still together, but really, we weren't. We had spent the past several months avoiding any drama that would have had an impact on our kids' daily routines. True to her word (and not surprisingly), Michelle remained a mother first and foremost throughout this time, putting the kids above whatever feelings she may have had about our situation. The two of us didn't talk a lot, but when we did, it was pleasant enough and usually centered around the kids. Truth be told, I was already living in the future. I was excited about what was to come.

Everything went smoothly on our trip. In fact, it served as a much-needed distraction from the complex day-to-day realities of our life back in Canada. Despite the awkwardness of bedtime, the trip also reminded me of how much I liked Michelle as a person and that we were just two people playing very strange roles in this weird game we'd found ourselves in. By the end of it, I felt incredibly proud of how we had handled these bizarre circumstances.

Upon arriving back in Toronto, we decided to wait a week for things to settle before talking to the kids. I was terrified at the thought of sharing the news and had no clue how they would respond. The week passed slowly, but finally, the big day arrived.

When I woke up, the first thought in my head was, *This is the day when I will officially come out. For real.* Once the kids knew, everything was fair game. The message would no longer be controlled, limited to only close friends and family in our circle of trust. From this day forward, the news would be released from the cage of secrecy and make its way freely throughout our little world. Knowing that felt both frightening and exhilarating.

When the kids got home from school that afternoon, Michelle and I told them we would like to speak with them together. They didn't seem to give it a second thought.

A few days before the big reveal, we'd met with a children's therapist to discuss our strategy for telling the kids the news. We were very concerned about both the short- and long-term damage that news like this might have on them. The therapist told us that how we delivered the news was important. We couldn't control what happened after that, but we could control how we framed the message. She also said that like most people, when kids receive news, their minds immediately go to how it will affect them. So we decided to be as factual as possible, to focus on assuring the kids that the only thing that would change in their lives was that I would be moving out. Everything else would remain the same.

Michelle and I planned to talk to the kids at seven so that they would have some time before bedtime—but not *too* much time. The minutes ticked by. We called the kids into the living room—the same living room where my wife and I had had the Big Talk six months before. We were both in different places now. She had gotten over the shock of my coming out and proceeded to move through other phases of grief as I was slowly getting to know this new part of myself.

When the clock struck seven, the kids arrived from different parts of the house. I noticed that we didn't need to call them more than once, which was unusual. Did they somehow sense the gravity of the occasion? Our three children sat down on the same brown sofa that Michelle had sat on when I told her the news. She sat on the sofa extension, and I stood, uncomfortably as usual, behind the coffee table at the far end of the room. Even though Michelle and I had agreed that we would tell them everything, I still couldn't fathom telling them the real reason our marriage was coming to an end. I tried to convince myself that it would be enough to tell them that we were separating. Many parents separate. The reasons don't matter.

"Mom and I want to tell you something about us," I heard myself say.

The kids raised their little eyes towards us, and I choked a little.

"You must have noticed that I've been sleeping in the basement for the past few months. Mom and I want to tell you that we are separating. I will move somewhere in the area to be close to you. Other than that, nothing will change for you guys. We love you very much."

The kids just sat there and said nothing.

"You have friends with divorced parents, right?" I prompted them.

All three nodded. And then nothing.

I was almost ready to end the conversation and open it up to questions when Michelle began talking. "And, you know, kids, the reason we're separating is that Dad is gay."

I could barely hold myself upright. I couldn't look the kids in their eyes. Tears sprang up in mine. *Fuck. She said it.* I knew it was the right thing to do, but still.

We asked the kids if they had any questions. There was silence for a while, and Michelle and I just sat there, giving them the space to begin to process all this information. I knew that there would be more questions in the future and that they needed the freedom and safety to ask those questions or to be angry or feel whatever other emotions they needed to feel. After a few minutes, our son, who was eleven at the time, said that he had a couple of questions.

"Of course. What do you want to know?" I asked. I figured he would ask about sexuality or maybe about where they would stay.

He had two questions. The first was: "Will we still have family dinners on Friday?" These Friday-night dinners were a long-standing tradition in our family. Every Friday, we got together with my parents, my brothers, and a couple of other friends who had become family over the years. My eyes met with Michelle. We didn't need to say anything to understand each other. We both nodded and promised that yes, we would still spend Friday nights together.

My son's second question was whether we would still go on family holidays together. Again, Michelle and I looked at each other and then said yes.

I don't think our son knew what he inadvertently did with those questions, but both of these activities have kept us together as a family in the years since that night. No matter what our issues or frustrations might be at any particular moment in time, we still meet every Friday. Those dinners and holidays are the invisible thread that has helped keep us together as a family. Sometimes we spend those Fridays with our new partners and sometimes it's just us, just like the old days.

Don't get me wrong. At first, these get-togethers felt a little odd. But with time, they became the new normal.

Our commitment to that promise to meet as a family on a weekly basis is the single thing that has kept our family together. During the first couple of years, Michelle and I had personal ups and downs. But even then, all the noise and commotion created by our family and friends distracted us from our personal issues for a couple of hours. And even though I could see that Michelle was going through a mourning period, it seemed like the loud energy of life eventually picked her up.

When the kids were younger, we even travelled together, except now we got two hotel rooms instead of one, with the boys and I in one room and Michelle and our daughter in the other. We even went on a trip of a lifetime to Africa several years down the line.

As the kids grew older, we gave up travelling together when it started to feel a little forced. But those trips and all that time we spent around the dinner table allowed us to discover what it meant to be a new kind of family.

CHAPTER NINETEEN

My New Life

Once I had moved everything into my new place, I happily sank down on my new not-so-practical sofa and looked around. It felt like my place. I walked down to a Korean supermarket on the main street and bought some fruits and vegetables for dinner. An hour later, I was sitting at my dining room table with a salad, drinking my second bottle of beer, with music playing on my new speaker system.

I was all alone, a little tipsy, and very happy.

My first year in the new apartment was great. Being out of the suburbs made me feel like I could breathe again. I visited all the cool breweries and indie galleries throughout the city. It was the type of area where people like me—people who couldn't afford the rent in the "good" areas—flocked to. The vibe felt right. It felt like me. I felt like me.

I also quickly discovered that for as much as I had felt confined by the routines of my life as a straight family man living in the suburbs, I still needed them in my new life. Now the routines just looked different because I based them on the things that mattered to me and added to my life. For example, since I love both coffee culture and walking and cycling, I built the routine of walking or riding to a different coffee shop every morning. As I visited the various coffee shops, I noticed how communal they were. It appeared that each shop was filled with the same group of regulars at the same time each day, many of whom seemed to know each other.

Since I am somewhat introverted and it was a challenge for me to start conversations with strangers, I decided to get to know the baristas. This was easy enough; I just made a habit of asking them questions about themselves. It's interesting how happy people are to share their passions or thoughts with a friendly stranger. With time, those baristas began asking me questions about myself in return, and thus coffee shop friendships were formed over time. I've met so many cool people this way: an art student who was excited about his next exhibition and a quirky shop owner who liked to ride his bike and take his boat out to the water during the summer months. I also made a point of giving these new friends some of our baked goods every once in a while. I realized how happy it made them that someone had thought about them and didn't want anything in return. I began to learn that we all crave human connection.

In addition to establishing myself in my new neighbourhood, I also spent those first few months getting to know myself as both a single guy and a gay man. I quickly realized that I had never really experienced being single as an adult. I discovered that I really liked spending time with myself. I was never lonely because I stopped by Michelle's house to have dinner with her and the kids a couple of times a week. It felt awkward initially, but I quickly realized that she wanted the kids to know that we were okay with each other, so I jumped on board. I give Michelle so much credit for this because it was clear that she wasn't just tolerating me but that she actually *wanted* me there. These dinners and time with the family also eased the transition from being married to being single. I didn't feel like I was free falling. I was still part of something.

The kids stayed at my place every other weekend. The first time they came over, they were very excited to see the building. Something as small as taking the elevators felt like a big adventure for them. Because I lived next to a main street, we could also walk places. Since I lived in a primarily Korean area of town, we spent a lot of time exploring the various Korean restaurants in the neighbourhood. The kids fell in love with a stand that sold a tasty dessert shaped like a fish and stuffed with sweet beans. The experience was so far removed from the life they knew in the suburbs that whenever the kids came to stay, they felt as if they were on holiday.

On the nights when I was alone, I would come home after work and stand at the balcony window, just looking at the world around me for a few minutes. I reviewed the day and allowed my mind to settle into relaxation. Then, I walked down to a local supermarket and bought just enough ingredients for one meal. This seemingly small act provided me with a sense of freedom. I didn't have to account for others, and I never knew what the following day would bring. Maybe I would make something different, or perhaps I would go downtown or visit friends. I was connecting to a slower pace of life. At last, my mind was no longer pre-occupied with blocking undesired thoughts or pretending to be someone I wasn't. Finally, the noise was gone, and I could release all the energy and effort that I had put into avoiding myself. With all this extra room, hope and a sense of possibility for the future had space to settle in.

At the same time I was getting to know myself, I was also getting to know what it meant to date as a gay man. On the apps, I lied about my age and said I was thirty-eight instead of forty-four. I tried to figure out the lingo, but I couldn't, so I left most of the questions on my profile unanswered. Maybe that added to my mysterious appeal? Or maybe guys don't really care what you write and are just concerned with the photo.

I had never held my physical appearance in high regard. Growing up, both of my brothers were good-looking. Aharon was tan with blond hair, and all the girls turned their heads when he walked by. Girls were always at our house wanting to spend time with him. Guy had darker skin and was also handsome. This was compounded by the fact that he was the captain of the soccer team and good at everything he did. Girls flocked to him too. As for me, I was always average: average looks and average in school. I was also extremely shy—not to mention critical of myself. Looking back, I probably would have done much better had I possessed more confidence.

This is all to say that my expectations for the hookup apps were low. While my experiences with Josh and my

Montreal date had been great for the purpose of stepping into this new world, they were short-term situations. I couldn't bring myself to go to a bar alone for the sole purpose of finding someone to hook up with. I *wanted* to, but my upbringing, shyness, or some combination of the two would not allow it. One big benefit to the apps was that they provided me with a sense of control over the situation. If I wanted, I could easily back away before anything happened. I could take my time getting to know someone until I got to the point where I was comfortable enough to meet up with him.

At first, I was the equivalent of the girl standing in the corner waiting for someone to ask her to dance. Then it suddenly occurred to me that I should probably send messages to others. The salesman part of me kicked in, and I said hello to as many guys as I could, providing they met my minimal standards. I didn't need everyone. I just needed one, and I was hedging my bets—cold calling, so to speak. After firing off several messages, I decided to put the phone down and go for a walk. It was too stressful sitting there, waiting for someone to reply. When I got back to my apartment, I walked directly to the phone, and to my surprise, there were five responses.

From that point on, I was out there.

Because I was now better able to understand myself and who I was, I also had a better understanding of what I needed in a partner and a willingness to stand up for myself in seeking that out. I quickly realized how important conversation and mental connection were to me in relationships, even in fleeting interludes. I wasn't interested in the sexual acts alone. I quickly discovered that I liked serial monogamy. I didn't like seeing more than one person at a time. So my relationships could last anywhere from a couple of days to three years.

Not everyone felt the same. I found that many guys only wanted one quick physical encounter and a minimal amount of talking. I quickly established a few ground rules for myself that allowed me to identify that type of guy. For instance, I never agreed to meet someone on the day we made first contact. I always got their phone number and carried our conversation from the app over to text. Before we met, I made sure I had access to some of their social media. Those were my guidelines, and most of the time, I followed them.

There was one time I broke my own rules. I came back to my apartment after having a few too many beers and hopped onto an app to see who was there. It turned out that I had drank more than I should have and fell asleep on my bed while I was scrolling.

I woke up to a knock on my door at two in the morning. Worried there was an emergency, I jumped to my feet and walked to the front door. "Who is it?" I yelled.

A man's voice responded and said my name. When I opened my door, he checked me out.

I know that look, I thought. *Fuck! I must have given him my address.* He was there for fun, but I really wasn't up for it. Even though I had apparently invited him over, my senses began taking control, and I was worried. I didn't want to be rude, though, so I let him in. My mind was scrambling, trying to figure out how I could get him to leave. I decided to pretend to be way more intoxicated than I was, which wasn't hard. Within ten minutes, I apologized to him and told him that nothing was going to happen because I was too drunk. In other words, "It's not you; it's me." That served as a good lesson about why I should stick to my ground rules.

Over time, I met a lot of great guys online. Some of those interactions were meaningless—they happened simply because we were either horny or lonely. But even behind all that loneliness and horniness, I engaged with real people and created some meaningful connections. Those encounters gave me the confidence I needed to explore this new world and my emerging self, even if they didn't mean much in the grand scheme of things.

After exploring this new and exciting world of dating for a whole year, I began getting tired of it. The excitement and thrill of the hunt had worn off, mostly because it wasn't much of a hunt. I could usually find someone else who was interested, but I was seeking a longer-lasting connection. I decided to get off the apps for a while and try to find a meaningful connection in other ways. Before I deleted the app, though, I decided to check my messages one last time. There was a message from Michael, someone I had said hello to before and hadn't yet heard back from. I decided to respond. Why not? We chatted a little and then moved our conversation to text. We decided to meet up.

When I drove home from work on the evening of our date, I didn't feel excited about going out. I didn't want another meaningless hookup. In fact, just the thought of it depressed me. Once I arrived home, I decided to cancel our meeting. I texted Michael and told him that I was sorry for wasting his time, but I'd decided not to meet up. I explained that I wasn't interested in another empty physical encounter. As I hit send, I figured that would be the end of that, and I felt relieved.

I began chopping my salad and thought how happy I was to be spending a no-pressure evening alone. About a half hour later, my phone dinged. It was Michael. He told me that it was fine if I wanted to cancel but that I should know we didn't have to hook up; we could just go out and get to know each other. He suggested we might go play board games and have a beer downtown.

This was different. I decided to meet him after all.

As I drove downtown, I couldn't help but feel excited about going on what felt like a proper date. And we had a great time, despite the fact that I lost every single game except for one (and I suspect that lone victory was a mercy win). With Michael, three hours felt like ten minutes.

From that night on, we began seeing each other. Michael was my first boyfriend after marriage, and our relationship lasted for three years. I got so much from our time together.

This new boyfriend marked the first time that my new life came together with my family life. Up to that point, the two had always remained separate. For the first several months of my relationship, I alternated weekends, with my kids staying one weekend and my boyfriend staying the next. Integrating these two worlds without compromising either of them was the final step for me.

When I began to strategize about what this would look like, my goal wasn't for everyone involved to love each other and want to spend every minute together. Initially, it was just for them to get to know one another and, hopefully, not hate each other. I would evaluate things from there, one step at a time.

First up was introducing Michelle to Michael after we'd been together for a few months. By that point, he was spending more nights at my place, and things were going well. It seemed like only a matter of time before he met the kids and maybe even spent the night while they were over. My policy with the kids was not to discuss my love life unless it was committed and stable. However, once I was dating someone seriously, I wanted them to be in the loop so they could be a part of it. I wanted to control the message and feel no shame about it. I figured they might feel uncomfortable the first few times they met a guy I was seeing, but beyond that, I wanted to make everything as comfortable and transparent as possible for them.

By this point, it had been about just over a year since I'd come out to the kids. During that time, I had moved from my first apartment to a new, very cool place located directly above a store in an up-and-coming neighbourhood close to downtown. When the kids came, we often bought a pizza and took it down to Trinity Bellwood Park to eat while sitting on the grass. After we finished eating, we always played Frisbee. The park was constantly buzzing with the young people who lived a little way down the street in a brand-new, massive condo complex. It seemed that the park served as the residents' living room and entertainment area. They sat out there in large circles, drinking cocktails concealed as pop, passing the drinks around the circle from one person to the next. Some played baseball on the east side of the park while others practiced walking on a tightrope strung up between two trees.

I figured this busy, happy, comfortable place was the perfect setting for my kids to meet my boyfriend.

I went into their first meeting with Michael with zero expectations other than to bring these two different and very important parts of my life together.

Just like we had so many times before, that afternoon, the kids and I headed down to the pizza shop to buy an extra-large pie. When it was ready, we walked over to the park and found an open space to claim as our own. As we settled in, I told them that my boyfriend was going to drop by and say hello. They didn't respond to the big news other than with a slight nod. Maybe they were trained to keep straight faces while receiving big news by this point. They didn't know that he was already at a coffee shop nearby, waiting for me to send a text telling him to come over. I didn't want to give the kids too much time to think about what was coming, and I knew that if they were anything like me, the pizza would definitely draw their attention away from any unwanted thoughts.

This was a big moment, revealing my boyfriend to the three most important people in my life. I saw Michael walking towards us across the grass, steering his bicycle alongside him. The Japanese characters that were tattooed on his arm were on full display, and I found myself hoping that ink would distract my kids from any other thoughts that might be going through their heads. I took a deep breath. *Here goes!* I reminded myself of how many murky waters I'd already swum through in the course of the past few years. I could navigate these waters as well. I knew by then that how I carried myself during and after the reveal set the tone for all of us.

I waved at Michael as he got closer. Three pairs of eyes moved up from the pizza to look in his direction.

Michael waved back with a big smile on his face that immediately made me smile in return, despite how nervous I was.

The kids remained silent and focussed on their pizza. I was purposefully chatty in hopes of putting everyone at ease. Not surprisingly, Michael was very engaging and tried to break the ice by asking the kids a couple of questions. As I watched Michael, I couldn't help but wonder how *he* was doing. After all, it's not every day that you meet your recently outed partner's three teenage kids. I was happy that everything seemed perfectly pleasant. After about twenty minutes or so, Michael got on his bike and rode off.

Mission accomplished, I thought. The goal was just to make this initial introduction so that moving forward, my kids and Michael could begin to interact naturally.

It wasn't until years later that my son told me that he'd thought I said they were meeting a friend, not a boyfriend, and that was why he didn't give that first meeting too much thought. I had to wonder if perhaps I subconsciously said the word "boy" very quietly.

From that point forward, Michael began staying over more often. When the kids stayed with us, we often went out to our favourite Chinese dim sum restaurant. One time, my father joined us too. I was so happy that my dad showed up in such a loving way. I have a photo of all of us sitting around the table. To this day it makes me happy every time I see it.

Another time when we were celebrating my birthday, Michelle joined Michael and me for dinner with the kids. The adults had a little bit to drink, and I was in seventh heaven over the fact that on my left was my wife (we were still separated but not divorced, so technically she was still my wife) and on my right was my boyfriend, and we were surrounded by our three wonderful kids. It's as if I have a gene in me that revels in being different.

By that point, the kids were teenagers, and they seemed to have adapted to this new family structure of ours. When I spent one-on-one time with them, I would try to chat them up about how they felt about everything and if there was anything I could do to support them. The boys had only told a couple of close friends about me. They told me that the words "faggot" and "gay" were derogatory in school. I told them that the kids who used those words either didn't know any better or might be dealing with internal conflicts caused by their own sexuality. The kids said that they didn't pay any attention to those kids and that they were okay. I was so happy to have these conversations with them.

I was (and still am) deeply proud of the fact that Michelle and I raised kids who saw the world through different lenses, which would make them more understanding and compassionate human beings.

CHAPTER TWENTY

The Price We Pay

To me, "being in the closet" doesn't resonate as an accurate description of what it felt like to bury my sexuality from everyone, including myself. It didn't feel as if I was locked in a small space, banging on the door to get out. Instead, denying my sexuality felt as if I was stuck in a huge, dark, and foreboding building, filled with long halls that led to many rooms. Each room contained its own collection of secret desires, shames, and loves. Late at night, my spirit floated around through the hallways like a ghost, peeking into all the rooms and gazing at the locked-in desires and secrets. As morning approached, my spirit buried itself deep down to hibernate in layers of shame.

Since I spent most of my time pretending to be someone else, I didn't have a North Star to keep me on track. I lived my life according to what I presumed other people thought I should be. I think that I'm quiet and shy by nature, but disconnecting from myself heightened that. I was hiding from myself, hiding from others, hiding from everyone. When you're hiding, you have to be quiet and remain as close to invisible as possible.

In a recent conversation with one of my childhood friends, I told him that I was thinking of doing a podcast. He went silent for a second or so and then he laughed. "Alon," he said, "that is the opposite of how you used to be. I can't remember you talking at all in school. I literally can't recall you speaking."

Now that I've stopped pretending to live a life that isn't mine as a person who isn't me, I don't care how others think I should behave. Quite the opposite, in fact. I want to be noticed and remembered now that I understand what it means to be in alignment with life and how that alignment impacts almost everything.

I feel a sense of lightness in my body and soul. I can talk with equal ease to complete strangers and those I love without caring what their response will be. Everyday life issues that used to require days and weeks of energy to deal with come and go in much shorter periods now. I'm able to brush off any comments or incidents that might offend me as opposed to allowing them to take root in a fertile ground of guilt and shame and blossom into even more negativity. I live a life that looks the way I want it to, do the things that I want to do, and say what I actually feel. If I'm at a dinner party and want to leave, I simply stand up, thank everyone, and leave. In recent years, I've been told that I'm selfish, but it's been said to me as a compliment and with a sense of envy by others who long to be freer.

Whereas the suburbs once felt as though they were designed with the sole purpose of crushing my soul, since coming out, my negative feelings about them have subsided. I still would never choose to live there because they're not me, but when I visit my friends who live in the suburbs, it strikes me as a nice, relaxing place to be.

Don't get me wrong. Of course, life still has its challenges, but now I can deal with them much better and more efficiently.

As a kid, this act of putting on a façade came naturally to me. It's not like I practiced not being me in front of a mirror. Acting like I was someone else was just something I did, to the point where I didn't even realize I was doing it. I often found myself unsure about what to say, so most times, I just didn't say anything at all. And when I did, my words didn't benefit anyone because they weren't really mine. They were just shallow thoughts stolen from people around me. I was like a tiny fish among a giant school, moving along with and mimicking the movements of the group.

Being like everyone else gave me a sense of safety. I figured that as long as I didn't stand out, there wasn't any risk. People wouldn't notice me or talk about me, but I could still have a false sense of belonging. That's what I wanted. We all need to belong to a group. Being part of a greater whole provides us with a sense of safety and familiarity; it gives us a sense of control over our lives. The majority of people achieve this sense of belonging by conforming (although not necessarily to the point I did). Of course, there is also a smaller group of people who define themselves by rebelling. They spend their energy opposing the norm, doing everything they can to look and sound different from others. They are not free either because they are defined by their *opposition* to the group. Then there are the artists, who channel the message that they need to channel. Many times, this message is stronger than the artists themselves, and suffering is involved. Finally, there is another group of individuals who do not conform to the group and who are colourful and unique, yet at the same time, they still love the group and want to belong. In my opinion, nirvana will occur at the point when all humans live in that way—when they can simultaneously embrace and bring into the world their authentic inner beauty while still accepting and loving others and being accepted and loved in return. I now understand that this desire, this need, was bubbling up inside of me for many, many years.

One time, Michelle and I were invited to a friend's birthday party over lunchtime in a restaurant event room. Our friend's family was there, including his wife's parents and a few other elderly people. At the time, I coped with events like this by drinking. On that particular day, I started drinking before the food was served. I've always been a lightweight drinker. It doesn't take much for me to get drunk, especially when I drink on an empty stomach.

That day, one beer followed another, and as the drinks flowed, I became louder and more obnoxious. Of course, I thought I was being cool at the time, but thinking back, I'm embarrassed by my behaviour. Halfway through lunch, I thought it would be funny to throw french fries at the birthday boy, who was sitting across the table, to get his attention. You can probably imagine that the fries made their way everywhere but where I intended them to go. I even landed a fry on my friend's father-in-law, which resulted in a very dirty look being shot in my direction.

When I see people behaving like this today, I know they must be going through something, and most likely, they're in escape mode. Because of that, I have some compassion towards them. Don't get me wrong; I will ask them to stop throwing fries, but I understand that my anger or frustration is the last thing they need.

Back then, pretty much every outing I went on at night involved extreme drinking. I just wanted to feel some semblance of happiness and forget my reality. I wanted to pump up the noise to block out the voices. I can't even begin to count the number of times I threw up while out and about. One time, I was riding on a subway car when I felt the drinks catch up with me. I felt so bad. Finally, my stomach couldn't take it any longer. Things are a bit blurry, but I remember taking the opportunity to vomit when the subway doors opened up at a stop. I pulled myself back into the car before the doors shut again and then repeated the process at the next stop. A few times, I had to throw up out of car windows while sitting in the passenger seat. I'm sure my behaviour was charming to everyone around me.

The worst instance of this drunken behaviour happened when I was living in the basement. One night, I went out and got trashed. I don't remember most of the night, but I do recall waking up on the floor and immediately being assaulted by a horrible stench. I heard my son call upstairs for Michelle to come down quickly. Soon after, I heard the door open and Michelle tell me to drag my ass over to the washroom. The room was spinning as I slowly got up. I made my way to the bathroom only thanks to the help of the basement walls. When I arrived, the stench was even stronger. I saw my son pointing at the sink, which was full of dry vomit. I felt so embarrassed that my kid had witnessed this. At that moment, I vowed never to throw up at home again. I still drank to the point where I threw up plenty—but never at home again.

After coming out, I found that my consumption of alcohol dropped dramatically. My body refused to drink after a certain point. My mind didn't need the distraction any longer.

I was only able to get that that point because with time, the voices in my head and waves of anxiety became so loud that no amount of noise I could create would drown them out.

Even though each of us is on our own unique journey, I know others who have reached crisis points in their lives due to inauthenticity, much like I did, and their mental and emotional states began to impact their physical state.

People who don't live their lives freely or authentically are like knotted-up hoses. The water gets stuck, and pressure builds up. More and more pressure builds over time, pushing against the walls of the hose. If those knots aren't undone, the hose will eventually burst. Only when the knots are untangled will the water begin to flow again.

These are the costs we pay for living a life that's not true to who we are. But if you can find the courage to break through that, there's so much to gain. *Everything* changes.

Today, I am very comfortable with myself. When I speak, the words are mine, and they are intentionally directed at the person in front of me. Sometimes, I still don't fit in. My brothers make fun of me and often tell me that my own personal brand of humour isn't very funny, but that doesn't stop me. My humour is from and for myself. It makes me smile, and that feels good.

I'm also comfortable in my own body. Sometimes my movements can be a little feminine. I've noticed that the way I carry myself changes a bit depending upon the environment I'm in, but that's a conscious choice. For example, I might be a bit more femme when I'm at a gay club with my boyfriend and more masculine when I'm walking through a dark alley late at night. This freedom to embrace different sides of myself while always remaining authentic is so liberating.

While not everyone's journey or circumstances look like mine, I've noticed that many people begin looking inward around the point in life when things calm down a bit—when the kids need you a little less, your career is more established, and there's suddenly a bit more breathing room to be with yourself. I've seen plenty of marriages negatively affected by this type of scenario. People realize that the husband or wife they picked fifteen years before isn't such a great match any longer. This can happen for any number of reasons. Perhaps one person experiences growth while the other does not, or maybe one of them discovers suppressed realities within themself as I did.

I also think that reaching the age of forty can have a significant effect on our perspective. Forty marks approximately the halfway point for the time we have here on this planet. Reaching that milestone makes many people realize,

Yikes! Life doesn't actually last forever! There is an end to this adventure. That realization can have a deep, thudding impact on those of us who are living inauthentic lives.

In my experience, blocking out these emerging realizations doesn't work. When I tried to ignore them, they only got louder. Rather than addressing the messages that were screaming to be heard, I began increasing the background noise by going out, travelling, and drinking at every chance I got. I slowly went from being the quiet, shy guy I had always been since I was a kid to being a partier. The problem was that the party had to continue constantly to prevent the internal noise from rising again.

When I came out, I released the knots I'd been carrying around my entire life. I was freed from all the bullshit I'd believed about myself. It brought my downward spiral to an end. With that freedom, I could breathe properly once again and was free to be just as I was. I believe the same is true for everyone. When we live in our truth, when we are true to who we are, everything else begins to flow. We heal.

For me, there were other benefits that I never expected. While my family's business had always seemed successful from the outside, it was hugely challenging from the inside. Over the years, we constantly invested our profits back into the company. We took low wages for a very long time—just enough to pay for our daily expenses. As our pay increased slowly over time, so did our lifestyles. In other words, the pressure never decreased.

We almost lost the business a couple of times when the winds turned against us. There were times when each of us had to take out an extra mortgage to bail the company out of trouble. Even as we did that, we weren't sure that things would turn out well. But we did it anyway because we believed in our business.

The first year after I came out, our business did really well. In fact, it was the first year that we each took a bonus. I had never before deposited a cheque that large. I knew deep down that it was this new authenticity and living in a way that was true to who I was supposed to be that had had this positive effect on other realms of my life.

When we got that bonus, my dad, Guy, and I decided to celebrate with dinner at a fancy steak restaurant downtown. It was one of those old-style steakhouses tucked away in an old brick building near the port. Everything around that building was changing. Skyscrapers were sprouting up from the ground all around it, but still, this building remained true to what it was, a capsule in time. The waiters dressed in black tuxedo pants, white button-down shirts, and black ties. They even mixed the Caesar salad on a trolley next to the table, something that hadn't been in vogue for the last thirty years or so. The three of us sat there in a nice, wooden booth, being served by an invisible arm that floated around us, pouring water and unfolding and placing white napkins on our laps.

This dinner felt particularly special to me because while I immediately knew that my brothers were good with this new version of me, it took some time for me to feel comfortable around my dad. It's not that my dad said or did anything to make me feel uncomfortable; it was all about my perception of how he was feeling and what he was thinking. Letting go of that took time.

My dad grew up in a different place, in a different era. In the course of his lifetime, he has seen society and technology change dramatically. In his traditional Jewish background, men were men, and women lived in the background, making sure the world continued to turn. Recently, my dad and I had a conversation about gay people who came of age in his time. He told me that he couldn't even begin to imagine how hard it must have been for them. He remembered a second cousin who got married and divorced within two weeks' time. My dad didn't know what had actually happened, but he remembered everyone whispering that his cousin was "different" behind his back.

Every time I was around my dad after I came out, I felt a little bit more comfortable chipping away at my old self and bringing out more of my new self (or, more accurately, the self I'd been hiding away for so long). To me, it felt as if our new relationship required mileage, and the only way to get those miles was to spend time together.

My dad and I have come a long way, but I will say that when my boyfriend and I visit my dad, I still feel uncomfortable demonstrating any physical affection or even sitting right next to my boyfriend. I'm aware that all of this is in my head. Sure, my dad may not be used to me touching a man in his home, but he would never say anything about it, and I imagine that with time, he would get used to it.

While these feelings of discomfort were strongest with my dad, I also sometimes felt similarly around other people. It was as if I needed to create a new version of reality for them and for myself, as if we needed to somehow create a new relationship. And that takes time.

Even after we find our truth and bring it into the world, it still takes practice and hard work. We have to realign our core with the people and reality surrounding us. This takes time.

In the years since coming out, I've seen a couple of life coaches. One of them told me that he believes in just being. Be who you are, and the rest will work itself out. I nodded my head in agreement when the coach said this, but now I understand it on another level.

Being starts from within. To truly be, we must learn to be aware of our surroundings without allowing who we are to be influenced by them. For most of my life, this was one of my biggest challenges. I found it difficult to get over how I thought people perceived me. But the more I came back to myself, the less I cared about what others thought.

A couple of years ago, my friend gave me a tank top with a coffee roaster's name printed on it in rainbow colours. I loved the tank top, but I didn't wear it until a few months ago because I worried it would be too revealing. One day, I decided to wear it. And...nothing. The world didn't skip a beat. If anything, I may have even gotten an extra smile or two thanks to my happy gay tank top.

CONCLUSION

I first started coming out a few years ago, and the process has never ended. I don't think it ever will. At first, it was my sexuality that needed to be set free. As I went through the process, I realized that the physical element of my sexuality was only a small part of what needed to come out. There was so much more I held tight under the surface. My expression, my movement, even the way I breathed—it all needed to come out. I needed to relax and just *be*.

One tool that has helped me the most is constantly executing a three-step process. I figure out where I want to go, and then I decide the next three steps I should take to get there. I take them with confidence—real or perceived, it doesn't really matter. I look at the gap in front of me and where I want to go. Then I determine the next three steps, and so on and so forth until I get to my destination. It's simple but not easy.

There are a select few people who are comfortable with who they are at an early age. But most of us are not. I think most of us need a coming-out process.

I believe this process of coming out is a challenge we take upon ourselves just before we are born. Our souls gather in a war room, surrounded by television screens. Each screen shows us a selection of potential lives and the challenges we will encounter. Once we choose a life, we commit to going through the challenges and pain that it brings with it. With this mission accomplished, we leave the world at least one step higher than it was when we entered.

When I see a fellow human suffering, the prayer that I always find emerging within me in response is: *please, God, help them learn their lesson quickly.* My prayer is not to obliterate the pain because often, it's necessary. The pain, and the challenges that come with it, ushers in growth and a greater trueness of self.

I needed to go through the pain to get to the other side. I was a slow learner. That's the main reason I wrote this book. Maybe you can learn a lesson from a slow learner.

EPILOGUE

The existence of this book is a testament to the fact that miracles do happen. Up until two years ago, I did not think that I could put more than a paragraph together. Yet a year ago, the words started flowing as if an underground dam had broken, and a flood of words and energy made its way to the surface. At first, the words formed short stories, and eventually, they became a memoir of sorts. Emotions, energy, thoughts, and love were all intertwined with those words.

I've found that between the ages of thirty and fifty, many people need to experience a coming-out process. In my case, it was the issue of my sexuality and living in the suburbs. For others, there is the "coming out" of the family they were born into and childhood realities and expectations. Sometime after the age of thirty, these issues can't be ignored any longer. It starts as a whimper that turns into a scream if ignored. It represents who we really are and need to be. The lucky ones change from caterpillars into the butterflies we are all meant to be. Once the transformation takes place, life becomes somewhat lighter; our step has more of a bounce to it, and energy goes with us more often than against us.

This book elevated my relationship with my ex-wife. At first, the personal nature of the book resurfaced emotional land mines that we were not aware existed. Pain and memories of what should have been overwhelmed us both. We gave ourselves time and communicated openly and clearly with each other. As a result, we got closer as the ex-partners and family we are. I'll forever be thankful for that.

I hope that this book will act as a North Star for you if you are in a place in life that feels wrong. If you feel that you are wearing someone else's skin and pretending to be someone you are not, may it wake you up to the inauthenticity that you have been living. May it give you the courage to break the chains and get to know the new/ real you.

Much love,
Alon

ACKNOWLEDGMENTS

This book was not born in a void. I am very fortunate to have supportive families and communities in my life. As I moved ahead on my path, new people and communities that supported the "new" me appeared.

I thank and acknowledge my ex-wife. I will always be there for you as you were for me. And my three amazing grown-up kids. I am the luckiest man!

Thank you to my close-knit family: brothers, father, and late mother. We have gone through a lot together. I love and appreciate you.

To my life partner. Your shoulder is the rock to lay my head on.

My love and gratitude go to all my friends, old and new, young and mature. I am truly blessed to have you in my life. You are the reason I haven't required much professional therapy. A beer/coffee and quality time together put the troubles of the day in perspective.

A big thank you goes to my second family of MMTs (Master Mind Talks). You are a big reason that my life keeps getting better. I never expected to meet such enlightened people!

I thank the people behind "One Last Talk," MMT, and Scribe for planting, watering, and nurturing the creation of this book. Without you this book would be a story anchored in the wind.

And last but not least, I thank you, the reader, for taking the time to read this book.

Thank you all for being patient with me. For being there and for holding the mirror in front of me. I know that I am a slow learner.

There's So Much More Than Straight or Gay

Because of the vast amount of information that our minds process, we human beings need clarity and gravitate towards one of two options. We understand male and female, masculine and feminine, black and white. In many older societies, male and female roles were clearly defined, and people had to fit in to their expected roles. There were no other options. How horrible was that for people who didn't fit in to one of these two neat categories? How much guilt, frustration, and shame must have built up inside of people who pretended to fit in and played the role of a different character their entire lives—acting during the day and burying their true selves when they were alone at night? How much anger and sadness resulted from those who felt different, like they didn't belong? They didn't know that there were others out there who were just like them. They didn't know that they were actually normal. The world was deprived of their full spectrum and beauty!

In thinking about this, I have mapped both the masculine and feminine energies and everything in between them. I'm not a researcher, but I am someone living in the midst of the laboratory we call life with keen and curious eyes.

The Old Country way of living gave us only two options:

Male: masculine, logical, in control, leading

Female: feminine, emotional, in need of guidance, following

Of course, now we know that, in reality, the spectrum is far more diverse than this. I have observed these subcategories in my own life and noticed that a person may be anywhere along the following spectrum:

GENDER SPECTRUM

Physical attraction
Attracted to women 1 _____ 10 Attracted to men

Behaviour/Energy
Masculine 1 _____ 10 Feminine

Processing/Language
Logical, scientific 1 _____ 10 Intuitive, emotional, artistic

This by no means covers all sexualities or modes of expression, but they are the perspectives that influence me.

As an example, one of my friends, whom I'll call John, is a strong, solid 1 in all three of these aspects. He is attracted to women. His behaviour is masculine. And he processes information in a purely logical manner. He is the straightest person I know.

Another friend of mine is attracted to women but open to experimenting with men. He falls somewhere in the middle between masculine and feminine in terms of behaviour and energy. His thought processing is somewhere between artistic and logical—I would give him a 5 on that scale. He's an artist who sees the world from both energies.

As for myself, I am a 7 on the physical attraction scale. I'm attracted to certain men but not all. I'm a 5 in both behaviour and processing.

This is to say that sexuality is about so much more than just straight and gay, and when we pretend it's not, we lose out on so much colour and so much beauty. Also, these gauges are not static; for some of us, they may shift with time as we grow, evolve, and become more familiar with our true selves. How beautiful would the world be if we allowed ourselves to just be who we are, no matter where we fall along these scales and no matter how contradictory some areas of that spectrum might seem to others? The beauty of it is that these gauges are not static.

Manufactured by Amazon.ca
Bolton, ON

23773949R00120